Trade Policy Review

GEORGIA
2009

World Trade Organization
Geneva, January 2010

WTO/GATT TRADE POLICY REVIEWS CURRENTLY AVAILABLE

Antigua and Barbuda	2001
Angola	2006
Argentina	1999, 2007
Australia	1989, 1994, 1998, 2002, 2007
Austria	1992
Bahrain	2000, 2007
Bangladesh	1992, 2000, 2006
Barbados	2002, 2008
Belize and Suriname	2004
Benin	1997
Benin Burkina Faso Mali	2004
Bolivia	1993, 1999, 2005
Brazil	1992, 1995, 2000, 2004, 2009
Brunei Darussalam	2001, 2008
Bulgaria	2003
Burundi	2003
Cameroon	1995, 2001
Cameroon and Gabon	2007
Canada	1990, 1992, 1994, 1996, 1998, 2000, 2003, 2007
Central African Republic	2007
Chad	2007
Chile	1991, 1997, 2003, 2009
China	2006, 2008
Colombia	1990, 1996, 2006
Congo	2006
Costa Rica	1995, 2001, 2007
Côte d'Ivoire	1995
Cyprus	1997
Czech Republic	1996, 2001
Djibouti	2006
Dominica	2001
Dominican Republic	1996, 2002, 2008
East African Community	2006
Ecuador	2005
Egypt	1992, 1999, 2005
El Salvador	1996, 2003
European Communities (European Union)	1991, 1993, 1995, 1997, 2000, 2002, 2004, 2007, 2009
Fiji	1997, 2009
Finland	1997
Gabon	2001
Gambia	2004
Georgia	2009
Ghana	1992, 2001, 2008
Grenada	2001
Guatemala	2002, 2009
Guinea	1999, 2005
Guyana	2003, 2009
Haiti	2003
Honduras	2003
Hong Kong, China	1990, 1994, 1998, 2002, 2006
Hungary	1991, 1998
Iceland	1994, 2000, 2006
India	1993, 1998, 2002, 2007
Indonesia	1995, 1998, 2003, 2007
Israel	1995, 1999, 2006
Jamaica	1998, 2005
Japan	1992, 1995, 1998, 2000, 2002, 2005, 2007, 2009
Jordan	2008
Kenya	1993, 2000
Kyrgyz Republic	2006
Liechtenstein	2000, 2004
Macao, China	1994, 2001, 2007
Madagascar	2001, 2008
Malawi	2002
Malaysia	1993, 1997, 2001, 2006
Maldives	2003, 2009
Mauritania	2002
Mauritius	1995, 2001, 2008
Mexico	1993, 1997, 2002, 2008
Mongolia	2005
Morocco	1990, 1996, 2003, 2009
Mozambique	2001, 2009
New Zealand	1990, 1996, 2003, 2009
Nicaragua	1999, 2006
Niger	2003
Nigeria	1991, 1998, 2005
Norway	1991, 1996, 2000, 2004, 2008
Oman	2008
Pakistan	1995, 2002, 2008
Panama	2007
Papua New Guinea	1999
Paraguay	1997, 2005
Peru	1994, 2000, 2007
Philippines	1993, 1999, 2005
Poland	1992, 2000
Qatar	2005
Republic of Korea	1992, 1996, 2000, 2004, 2008
Romania	1992, 1999, 2005
Rwanda	2004
Saint Kitts and Nevis	2001
Saint Lucia	2001
Saint Vincent and the Grenadines	2001
Senegal	1994, 2003
Sierra Leone	2005
Singapore	1992, 1996, 2000, 2004, 2008
Slovak Republic	1995, 2001
Slovenia	2002
Solomon Islands	1998, 2009
Sri Lanka	1995, 2004
Sweden	1995
Switzerland and Liechtenstein	1991, 1996, 2000, 2004, 2008
Separate Customs Territory of Taiwan, Penghu, Kinmen and Matsu	2006
Southern African Customs Union	1998, 2003, 2009
Tanzania	2000
Thailand	1991, 1995, 1999, 2003, 2007
Togo	1999, 2006
Trinidad & Tobago	1998, 2005
Tunisia	1994, 2005
Turkey	1994, 1998, 2003, 2007
Uganda	1995, 2001
United Arab Emirates	2006
United States	1990, 1992, 1994, 1996, 1999, 2001, 2004, 2006, 2008
Uruguay	1992, 1998, 2006
Venezuela	1996, 2002
Zambia	1996, 2002, 2009
Zimbabwe	1995

Co-Published by the World Trade Organization and Bernan Press. Printed in the U.S.A.

ISBN 13: 978-1-59888-387-9
ISSN: 1556-2050

All reports are available in English, French, and Spanish.

For more information, please contact:

WTO PUBLICATIONS
Centre William Rappard
Rue de Lausanne 154
1211 Geneva 21, Switzerland
Telephone: (41 22) 739 5208, 5308
Fax: (41 22) 739 5792
Email: publications@wto.org
www.wto.org

BERNAN PRESS, a wholly owned subsidiary of
The Rowman & Littlefield Publishing Group, Inc.
4501 Forbes Boulevard, Suite 200
Lanham, MD 20706, U.S.A.
Telephone: (301) 459-7666 (Washington, D.C. area)
(800) 865-3457 (toll-free)
Email: info@bernan.com
www.bernan.com

PREFACE

The Trade Policy Review Mechanism (TPRM) was first established on a trial basis by the GATT CONTRACTING PARTIES in April 1989. The Mechanism became a permanent feature of the World Trade Organization under the Marrakesh Agreement which established the WTO in January 1995.

The objectives of the TPRM are to contribute to improved adherence by all WTO Members to rules, disciplines and commitments made under the Multilateral Trade Agreements and, where applicable, the Plurilateral Trade Agreements, and hence to the smoother functioning of the multilateral trading system, by achieving greater transparency in, and understanding of, the trade policies and practices of Members. Accordingly, the review mechanism enables the regular collective appreciation and evaluation of the full range of individual Members' trade policies and practices and their impact on the functioning of the multilateral trading system. It is not intended to serve as a basis for the enforcement of specific obligations under the Agreements or for dispute settlement procedures, or to impose new policy commitments on Members.

The assessment carried out under the TPRM takes place, to the extent relevant, against the background of the wider economic and developmental needs, policies and objectives of the Member concerned, as well as its external environment. However, the function of the review mechanism is to examine the impact of a Member's trade policies and practices on the multilateral trading system.

Under the TPRM, the trade policies of all Members are subject to periodic review. The four largest trading entities in terms of world market share, counting the European Communities as one, are reviewed every two years, the 16 next largest trading entities every four years, and other Members every six years; a longer period may be fixed for least-developed countries.

The reviews are conducted by the Trade Policy Review Body (TPRB) on the basis of two documents: a policy statement by the Member under review and a comprehensive report drawn up by the WTO Secretariat on its own responsibility.

TABLE OF CONTENTS

Note: The documents that comprise this publication are available online at: http://www.wto.org/english/tratop_e/tpr_e/tp_rep_e.htm.

PART A

CONCLUDING REMARKS BY THE CHAIRPERSON

OF THE TRADE POLICY REVIEW BODY,

H.E. MR. ISTVAN MAJOR

AT THE TRADE POLICY REVIEW

OF GEORGIA

8 AND 10 DECEMBER 2009

CONCLUDING REMARKS BY THE CHAIRPERSON

1.   This first Trade Policy Review of Georgia has given us a much clearer understanding of the evolution of Georgia's trade policies since its accession to the WTO, together with the challenges it faces. I thank Ms Kovziridze and her delegation and I would also like to acknowledge the valuable contribution of the discussant, Mr Krzysztof Januszek of Poland, and of Members for their active and insightful participation in this exercise. The reports by the Georgian authorities and the Secretariat, as well as the detailed responses of the delegation of Georgia to the many questions posed, have contributed to transparency both within Georgia and as far as the WTO membership is concerned.

2.   Members commended Georgia's commitment to openness in trade and foreign investment as well as recent progress in economic liberalization. Members praised Georgia for its impressive economic performance during most of the review period, with an average annual GDP growth rate of 9-10%, in considerable part due to reforms, which have been widely recognized. In particular, important trade reforms have taken place in the areas of tariffs, improvement of Customs, business licensing and the adoption of trade legislation compatible with international standards. Nonetheless, Georgia has only partially succeeded in improving the external competitiveness of the private sector and, in this regard, Georgia was encouraged to continue its structural reforms to make its markets more flexible, attract investment into export activities, improve productivity and competitiveness, and thereby help sustain growth.

3.   Members congratulated Georgia on its liberal trade regime with its simple tariff structure and one of the lowest average applied MFN tariff rates in the world whilst almost 85% of imports enter Georgia duty-free. It was also noted that Georgia had not resorted to any restrictive measures since the onset of the economic crisis. Georgia's commitment to the WTO system was emphasized and Georgia was urged to follow through on its readiness to join the Government Procurement Agreement. Georgia was also encouraged to enhance WTO notifications in a number of areas. Regarding alignment with international standards and practices, Members noted that there is room for improvement in a number of areas such as SPS, technical regulations, competition policy and intellectual property rights enforcement, which point to the broader, more long-term problem of capacity building in general.

4.   Members noted that exports, which account for about one-fifth of Georgia's GDP, have not matched the strong overall economic growth rate in the review period. Georgia's main exports remain concentrated in a few low-value added products, reflecting limited success in efforts to diversify exports. Members were interested to know from Georgia the policies and measures it proposes to take to enhance its exports in the coming years.

5.   Members appreciated the replies provided by the delegation of Georgia and looked forward to further responses. In conclusion, the numerous questions and active discussion indicate the importance Members attach to this Review. I encourage Georgia to take to heart Members' concerns and I hope it will continue with its reform process which has resulted in strong economic performance and has helped the country to become a significant regional trade corridor. At the same time I invite Members to assist Georgia by providing appropriate technical assistance, including trade capacity building, and by further opening their markets to Georgia's exports.

PART B

REPORT BY THE WTO SECRETARIAT

This report was drafted by Mario Kakabadse
under the supervision of Michael Daly.

Richard Eglin
Director
Trade Policies Review Division

CONTENTS

Page

Page

SUMMARY OBSERVATIONS

(1)   ECONOMIC ENVIRONMENT

1.   Georgia, a small, strategically located middle-income country of 4.5 million people in the South Caucasus, had an estimated per capita income of US$2,900 in 2008, over three times its level at the beginning of the review period in 2003, when sustained growth resumed following many years of economic decline.   After independence in 1991, the Georgian economy collapsed under the impact of civil war and the loss of preferential access to Former Soviet Union (FSU) markets, output falling by 70% and exports by 90% in the worst decline suffered by any transition economy.

2.   Since 2003, economic policies have met with considerable success, guided by reliance on the private sector for growth in a liberalized trade, investment, and business environment;   the World Bank recognizes Georgia as one of the world's fastest reforming economies.   Prior to the armed conflict with Russia of August 2008, the economy was growing strongly, with real GDP rising by nearly 10% per annum on average. Underlying this has been a substantial increase in the tax to GDP ratio, a rapidly improving business climate and increasing inflows of foreign direct investment (FDI), which more than doubled from 8.4% of GDP in 2003 to an estimated 17.2% in 2007.   FDI inflows rose strongly at first due to the construction of oil and gas pipelines and since 2005 investment has flowed into infrastructure, construction, retail services and real estate, causing domestic demand for construction materials, food and consumer goods to boom   although domestic production of these inputs has not kept pace.

3.   The rapid economic growth since 2003 has not been associated with growth of exports relative to GDP.   The share of exports remained moderately low at about 20%, less than half the share of imports, which reached 49% of GDP in 2008, in part reflecting relatively limited investment in export-oriented agri-business and manufacturing industries.   Although there has been some diversification, Georgia's export structure remains quite concentrated in traditional products such as base metals, prepared foodstuffs, mineral products, chemical products, machinery and cement. Furthermore, the recent economic growth has largely been job neutral in net terms, as high quality private-sector job created have just about compensated for job cuts resulting from public-sector reforms.   The unemployment rate rose from 12.6% in 2002 to 16.5% in 2008. Poverty remains widespread, at an estimated 22.1% in 2008, most of the poor are in rural areas where livelihoods continue to rely on low-productivity subsistence agriculture.

4.   In 2008, the economy was hit by the twin shocks of the brief but disastrous armed conflict with the Russian Federation in August and the global financial crisis in September, which brought about a collapse in export demand, a reduction in FDI and worker remittances, and a sharp contraction in bank lending.   With the sudden drop in capital inflows and the onset of a credit drought, the economy contracted in the second half of the year with GDP growth for the full year of only 2.1%.   In the first quarter of 2009, the downturn continued as the economy contracted by 5.9%. Damage from the conflict to infrastructure, and disruption to activity in several sectors – including construction, trade, and tourism – severely dampened economic growth.

5.   Inflation was maintained in single digits through most of the review period but crept into double digits late in 2007 largely due to rising energy and food prices. Inflation slowed considerably in 2008 as global commodity prices receded and domestic demand contracted, given the central bank's focus on tightening monetary policy to contain inflation pressures in the first half of 2008. End-period inflation was 5.5% for 2008 and, according to the authorities, 12-month inflation was only 2.3% at end-June 2009.

6.   Georgia's large current account deficit, which reflects high gross domestic investment relative to national savings, expanded as a percentage of GDP from 6.9% in 2004 to 22.8% in 2008. The deficit has been covered by the surpluses in the capital and financial accounts, mainly due to large FDI inflows. Current account developments have been dominated by rapid import growth due to growing domestic demand, FDI-related imports, and rising energy and commodity prices. The merchandise trade deficit nearly doubled during the review period, from 16% of GDP in 2003 to 30% by 2008. Balance-of-payments data for the first half of 2009 show that exports and imports of goods declined by 35% and 38% respectively (compared with the first six months of 2008), which reflects a fall in commodity prices as well as reduced domestic demand.

(2)   TRADE AND INVESTMENT POLICY FRAMEWORK

7.   By the time of its accession to the WTO in 2000, Georgia had established the legislative basis for competitive markets by liberalizing its trade and investment regimes, freeing prices, rescinding exclusive rights granted to certain economic agents, abolishing restrictions on competition, privatizing state-owned enterprises, and cutting subsidized credits to state-owned enterprises. Policies pursued during the review period have built on these achievements in particular in the trade area: in tariff reform, combating corruption in Customs, reform of the business licensing sector, regulatory reform of the financial sector, and the continuing adoption of trade-related legislation compatible with European and international standards, including in the area of standards and technical regulations, food safety, and competition. These, together with the Law on Investment Activity Promotion and Guarantees, and the Law on State Promotion of Investments, have helped open the economy and create a business environment favourable to foreign investment.

8.   Trade policy formulation and evaluation are under the overall responsibility of a governmental commission headed by the Prime Minister. The PM's office is also in charge of the negotiations and matters relating to the WTO and the EU-Georgia FTA process, Georgia's main bilateral trade relationship. Foreign trade and related issues fall largely under the purview of the Ministry of Economic Development (MoED). Other line ministries and agencies such as the Ministry of Agriculture, the Ministry of Finance (including Customs) also play an important role in trade policy formulation and implementation.

9.   Georgia has MFN trading relationships with all WTO Members and has GSP arrangements with Japan, Canada, Norway, the United States, and Switzerland. In 2008, GSP-plus privileges granted by Turkey were replaced by a Georgia-Turkey FTA, under which customs tariffs on industrial products have been fully eliminated, although a number of agricultural products are excluded by both parties. In 2007, Georgia and the United States signed a Trade and Investment Framework Agreement, and in January 2009 Georgia signed the Georgia-U.S. Charter on Strategic Partnership, which, *inter alia* updates the bilateral investment treaty, expands Georgian access to the GSP, and explores the possibility of a free-trade agreement.

10.   Georgia has a free-trade regime with the (other 11) members of the Commonwealth of Independent States, which have traditionally been Georgia's largest trade partners, and although their share of trade with Georgia has declined, they still accounted for 36% of exports and 33% of imports in 2008. In August 2009, Georgia terminated its membership of the CIS organization while maintaining its right to remain a member the CIS free-trade area arrangements and the bilateral agreements with CIS members. In 2005 and 2006, Russia banned imports of Georgian agricultural products, mineral water, and wine, for which Russia was Georgia's largest market. In September 2006, Russia cut all direct transport links with Georgia and

doubled the price of natural gas supplied to Georgia. Since the August 2008 armed conflict, Russia has consolidated its position in Abkhazia and South Ossetia, confirming the *de facto* removal of about one fifth of Georgia's customs territory from central control.

11. Georgia enjoys GSP-plus status with the European Communities, enabling it to export about 7,200 items to the EC market with zero tariff rates. Previously Georgia was allowed to export only 3,300 products without any customs duty and 3,900 products under certain preferences. In December 2008, the EU announced plans to enhance its relationship with Georgia (as well as Armenia, Azerbaijan, Moldova, and Ukraine) as part of a new Eastern Partnership, which will involve gradual integration into the EU economy for countries that are willing and able to enter into a deeper engagement. The new partnership builds on the European Neighbourhood Policy framework, which has heavily influenced Georgian trade policy since 2006 and envisages progressive regulatory approximation of Georgia's legislation and practises to the most important EU trade-related regulatory policy *acquis,* as well as the negotiation of a deep and comprehensive free-trade area. In many areas, Georgian legislation is already close to that of the EU.

(3) TRADE POLICIES AND PRACTICES

12. Regarding measures affecting imports, Georgia has streamlined and liberalized its tax, customs, and tariff regimes. A new customs code entered into force in 2007, aimed at simplifying customs procedures and harmonizing both customs legislation and procedures with the European Community Customs Code and the revised Kyoto Convention. The current average applied MFN tariff rate is 1.5%, down from 7.2% in 2005, making it one of the lowest worldwide. The number of tariff bands was reduced from sixteen to three (0%, 5%, and 12%) with a maximum tariff of 12%. Nearly 86% of imported goods enter duty-free compared with

26% in 2005; agricultural goods and construction materials are the main items taxed at the higher rates. Over 98% of tariff lines are *ad valorem* rates, and 183 lines are subject to specific duties, mainly comprising alcoholic beverages, excluding beer. Georgia has bound all its tariffs. The average bound MFN rate is 7.5%, which affords only limited latitude to Georgia to raise its tariffs within existing bindings, and the authorities state that applied rates have not been raised during the review period. The majority of tariff lines at the 12% applied rate are bound at 12% (although tobacco is bound at 30%, the highest rate). There is effectively no tariff escalation nor any evident international tariff peaks.

13. In addition to the customs tariff, the Georgian authorities apply VAT of 18% and excise taxes on imported goods; in principle these apply equally to domestically produced and imported goods. Higher excise duties on imported tobacco are the exception, although the Government notes that it intends to equalize the rates on tobacco products.

14. The contribution of tariffs to overall tax revenue has decreased, in relative terms, in line with the decline in the effective import tariff rate, falling from 32% to under 3% between 1998 and 2008. However, excise taxes and VAT collected on imports have ensured that taxes affecting trade have maintained their significant share, of around one third of total tax revenue. Excise taxes on imports have maintained a relatively constant share of around 22% whereas VAT collected on imports now accounts for the lion's share of taxes on imports. A fixed customs fee also applies to imports.

15. Customs valuation for imports is administered in accordance with the revised customs code on the c.i.f. value of the goods. The authorities note that over 90% of all goods (except cars, which are cleared according to fixed rates) are cleared using the transaction value method. The origin of goods may be non-preferential (where Georgia adheres to WTO rules related to the determination of

country of origin) or preferential (where Georgia differentiates between CIS countries, GSP preferences, and rules of origin under the FTA with Turkey). In accordance with the revised customs rules, pre-shipment inspection has been abolished.

16. Georgia does not apply contingency measures and has not elaborated the relevant legislative basis for such measures. Georgia has no quantitative restrictions on trade. The import licensing system was simplified in 2005 when the number of licences required for import and export was reduced from 14 main groups to 8, with licensing objectives limited to protecting public health, the environment, and national security.

17. Georgia is an observer to the WTO Agreement on Government Procurement and in principle welcomes membership. The 2005 Law on State Procurement applies to the procurement of all goods, works, and services funded from state and local budgetary resources by about 3,500 procuring entities. Under the law, government procurement, which accounts for about one sixth of GDP, has been liberalized with the phasing out of preferences for domestic bidders, granted to promote the development of domestic contracting and manufacturing industries. Legislative amendments currently under parliamentary consideration aim to increase transparency (and thus reduce discretion and corruption) through the introduction of electronic procurement.

18. There are minimal export restrictions in terms of export taxes or licensing, no export subsidies nor any government financing for exporters other than bank loans at market interest rates.

19. On acceding to the WTO Georgia committed itself to adopting a new standards system comprising voluntary standards and mandatory international technical regulations to replace the Soviet system of mandatory standards. Under 2005 reforms, in order to meet the requirements of the WTO and align

the system to international practice, legislative changes were made to, *inter alia,* facilitate the transposition from a mandatory to a voluntary standardization system, the introduction of technical regulations, and the establishment of a standards agency. Adoption of new national standards, based on international (mainly ISO) and European standards, has made significant progress over the past two years. Regarding SPS requirements, Georgia has made major legislative and institutional changes in its transition from a centrally planned to a market economy, and although it has adopted a number of new laws covering food safety, veterinary, and plant protection issues, minimum international standards for food safety have not yet been achieved and the sector lacks funding to ensure adequate nationwide food-safety structures. For example, the 2005 law on Food Safety and Quality has been amended twice, resulting in the suspension of the law's core articles, due to insufficient institutional capacity and fear of factory closures in the food industry because of financial inability to meet the legal requirements.

20. The business environment has undergone a sea change in recent years with the number of business activities subject to licences and permits reduced by over 80% since 2005; this has been important in attracting foreign investment. In addition, special taxation regimes for international financial companies, international companies operating in free industrial zones, and free warehouse companies, exempt them from profit and property tax. Significant privatization of state-owned enterprises has occurred in recent years with the government receiving over US$1.4 billion in revenue between 2005 and 2008 from the telecommunications, energy, and health sectors, and large-scale real estate. Competition law was overhauled in 2005 with the focus on the prohibition of state aids and subsidies although, in the view of some observers, the law does not apply sufficiently to agreements restricting competition, concerted practices, abuse of dominant

position in the market, takeovers and mergers, and state enterprises. Some sector-specific anti-monopoly regulations are enforced through independent national regulatory commissions in key sectors, including energy, water supply, communications, transport, and financial services.

21.   Intellectual property legislation covers several IP areas including patents, trade marks, copyright, and geographical indications, but continuing resource and capacity constraints appear to be the main hindrances to effective implementation.   There is a generally acknowledged lack of capacity in law-enforcement bodies and the judiciary system to deal with IPR infringements, which is not uncommon for post-Soviet countries. There is no special IPR unit in the police and there is a lack of coordination among the different enforcement agencies.   Currently, the authorities in Georgia do not have *ex officio* powers to enforce IPR protection, except for Customs regarding IP objects listed in the Customs Register. A lack of data makes it difficult to estimate the extent of pirated and counterfeit products in Georgia, although the Government, with the assistance of UNDP is carrying out a study to better assess the volume of pirated and counterfeit products in circulation

(4)   SECTORAL POLICIES

22.   Georgia's economy has undergone significant structural change since Independence, when shares of agriculture, industry, and services in GDP were more or less evenly split. The share of agriculture has since declined significantly to an estimated 10.3% of GDP in 2008 although the sector remains critical for the economy: 53% of the labour force continues to rely on (subsistence) agriculture and the sector accounts for 18% of exports, although Georgia's net trade in agriculture and food products remains negative. Labour productivity in agriculture is barely one tenth of that in the rest of the economy, generating low incomes and thus poverty with rural areas accounting for 59% of

the total poor in the country and 62% of the extreme poor.   Among the reasons for agriculture's decline, are a shortage of credit, which has prevented farmers from purchasing high-quality seeds and fertilizers, and the small size of land plots, which prevents economies of scale and discourages mechanization.

23.   Key agricultural policies carried out in recent years include land reform, privatization of farms and agri-industry, facilitating access to finance, attracting investment, and use of open trade policies. Imports of agricultural products are subject only to tariffs (0%, 5% or 12%) and sanitary and phytosanitary measures. The binding coverage for agricultural products is 100%, and Georgia has rather low tariff rates on most agricultural products with the exceptions of sugars and confectionary, beverages, and tobacco. There is no special export regime applicable to agricultural goods, no export credits other than those available from commercial banks, and no system of export credit guarantees or insurance cover arranged by the Government. Georgia bound its agricultural export subsidies at zero when it acceded to the WTO and there are no export subsidies in place.

24.   Georgia has adopted a number of laws covering food safety, veterinary, and plant protection matters. The authorities maintain that minimum international standards for food safety have been satisfied at the legislative level, and that the Government is in the process of elaborating a comprehensive food safety strategy, which is being drawn up in line with EU standards. Challenges that need to be met include the gap between the quality of inspection and testing and the requirements of international standards, the organization and responsibilities of inspection bodies and laboratories, the risks for consumers due to food-borne diseases, and the lack of slaughterhouses, which undermines food safety and meat production.

25.   Industry,   comprising   mining, manufacturing, utilities and construction,

contributed 21.7% of GDP in 2008 and provided employment to 10.5% of the total employed labour force in 2007, making labour productivity more than twice the level in the rest of the economy. The most significant parts of the sector are the agri-processing and energy industries. During most of the review period, the performance of manufacturing industry has shown double-digit growth, driven both by external demand for certain goods, mainly metals, cement, and fertilizers, and by increased domestic demand for processed foods, soft drinks, building materials, and timber. The Government has not prioritized any sectors with regard to industrial policy; its overall policy is to minimize state intervention in the market and to promote a business-friendly environment through economic and institutional reforms, which have helped to create a favourable investment climate. To enhance productivity growth and competitiveness, the authorities have pursued structural reforms on several fronts, including trade liberalization, privatization, enterprise, business regulatory and institutional reforms, and in the area of standardization and in labour regulations.

26. During the review period, Georgia, a net energy and fuel importer, made good progress in energy sector reforms to address chronic power shortages and the poor financial state of electricity and gas companies. The electricity and gas markets for industrial users were liberalized in 2006 and 2008 respectively. The Government has completed the privatization of assets in power generation and distribution. The main objectives of energy policy are diversification of supply sources (to include harnessing the full potential of domestic hydropower resources), liberalization and deregulation of the market to attract competitive private investment, and the maximization of Georgia's benefits as an energy transit corridor. Moving towards more energy independence is critical given that energy imports, mainly oil and gas, accounted annually for nearly one fifth of the total import bill during the review period, a significant

contributory factor to the country's large trade deficit.

27. Services accounted for approximately 69% of Georgia's current GDP in 2008, up from 56% in 2002 and around 32% in 1998. Employment in the services sector remained more or less constant at about 37% of total employment during the period under review, indicating a marked improvement in labour productivity. Georgia has a small surplus on the balance of services within the current account, mainly reflecting income relating to oil and gas pipelines. Georgia's position in the services negotiations in the Doha Round is that it has unilaterally liberalized the services sector and therefore it has not made an initial offer.

28. The financial sector is growing rapidly but is still among the smallest relative to GDP in the Europe and Central Asia region, and remains dominated by banks. Virtually all financial intermediation takes place through the banking system, meaning that the mobilization and transformation of financial resources into investment is carried out by banking institutions rather than the underdeveloped capital market. Georgia completed the privatization of its banking sector in 1995 and since then has maintained no restrictions on foreign ownership of banks. Foreign investment in the sector is significant, accounting for 75% of total bank capital in 2009, up from 36% in 2005. Effective prudential regulation of the banking sector has contributed significantly to its rapid growth. For a decade or more, Georgia has maintained a simple bank licensing regime, under which only one type of bank licence exists, allowing licensed banks to engage in all banking activities and preventing excessive fragmentation of the sector, which may happen with several types of banking licences. Georgian banks were allowed to pursue a universal banking model with the leading banks becoming involved, through acquisitions, in insurance, broker-dealer activities, wealth management, pensions, card processing, and related activities.

29.   In March 2008, Parliament approved the Global Competitiveness of the Financial Services Sector Act to modernize the financial sector including: establishing a single Financial Supervision Agency (FSA) for the banking and non-banking sectors, although this is currently under review; strengthening the independence of the Central Bank, which will focus more on inflation targeting; demutualizing the stock exchange; and developing an international financial centre to attract foreign funding by offering tax exemptions to large international financial companies whose activity in Georgia does not exceed 10% of their financial turnover.

30.   In the telecommunications sector, all market segments including local, domestic long-distance, international long-distance, mobile, data, and internet are formally liberalized. However, there appears to be little competition, with fixed-line services dominated by the incumbent operators. The mobile telephone industry has been growing rapidly: in 2008, three mobile telephony operators provided services for over 2.7 million subscribers, up from 430,000 subscribers in 2002. Competition between these operators has stimulated considerable growth in the market and the authorities state that there are no legislative or financial entry barriers for companies to enter the market. Georgia's communications sector is currently regulated by the Georgian National Communications Commission (GNCC) and governed by the Law on Electronic Communications. The law was adopted in 2005 and, according to the authorities, is in compliance with the five EU communications directives.

31.   As a strategic transit corridor for pipelines carrying Caspian oil and natural gas to world markets, Georgia has an important role in existing and planned projects for the transportation of oil and natural gas along the South Caucasus transit system outside the territory of the Russian Federation and Iran. While this yields only modest revenue in transit fees, its main importance is in helping

Georgia to establish itself as a guarantor of western energy security. Georgia's non-oil-transit potential remains largely untapped; it accounts for a relatively small share of the non-oil trade of the Central Asian republics and of Armenia and Azerbaijan. Factors that contribute to underperformance include poor road conditions and high transit times. Road infrastructure improvement is one of the Government's stated priorities and several projects are under way in conjunction with several donors and international institutions.

32.   During the Soviet period, mass tourism was a major industry for Georgia with around 5 million visitors a year mostly from various parts of the FSU. Tourist numbers are now only a fraction of what they were but nevertheless expanded more than three-fold during 2000-08 from 387,000 to nearly 1.3 million. Around 60% of Georgia's foreign tourists still come from the CIS, and tourists coming from Turkey now account for more than a quarter of total arrivals. However, the share of higher-spending tourists from OECD countries have seen their share of arrivals decline to almost insignificant levels. Tourism-related investments have seen impressive growth in recent years, reaching over US$1 billion in 2008. In terms of policies to encourage and develop tourism, procedures for issuing visas to visitors have been simplified and the tax code adjusted so that tour operators' incoming tourist revenue from the beginning of 2006 has been exempted from VAT. However, a recent wide-ranging review of tourism policies, institutions, and infrastructure found substantial tourism potential but also serious impediments in terms of room stock, access to sights and attractions, and infrastructure.

(5)   OUTLOOK

33.   The on-going global economic crisis continues to threaten Georgia's growth prospects; lower commodity prices (in particular for fertilizers and metals), a drop in demand for Georgian exports, and a significant decline in private capital inflows

from abroad, which have been the main driver of growth, all negatively affect the economy. The Georgian authorities forecast a contraction for 2009 of at least 1.5%, and the IMF has revised its 2009 growth projections for Georgia downwards and anticipates a contraction in real GDP for the year of around 4%, taking into account the declines in private capital inflows, exports and remittances, as well as delays in official assistance and possibly prolonged regional political tensions.

34.   Exports and imports of goods and services are projected to decline by 20% and 27% respectively, reflecting flat import volumes, and lower world oil prices, which will bring down the oil import bill.   In addition, exchange rate depreciation is likely to discourage growth in consumer imports. On the other hand, the slowdown in trading partners is likely to keep exports subdued in 2009, neutralizing the potential boost from a lower exchange rate.   In particular, lower world demand for key commodity exports, such as copper and other metals, will dampen export earnings.   FDI inflows, hitherto the main source of financing for the current account deficit and a principal driver of economic growth, are projected to be in the region of US$900 million for 2009, 40% lower than in 2008, depriving the economy of a significant source of growth. Flows of workers' remittances have also decreased as

Russia (where the majority of Georgians working abroad are based) experiences a recession.

35.   Provided that some regional stability is restored, the Georgian economy should experience higher growth rates from 2010, based on an expected recovery in exports and a significant recovery in FDI.   Real GDP growth is forecast at 2% in 2010, with the level of potential growth in the medium term remaining uncertain.   Inflation is expected to remain moderate at 3-5% in the medium term due to declines in credit from the banking sector and world commodity prices. The large amount of external aid granted to Georgia in the aftermath of the armed conflict could stimulate higher rates of consumption and investment, bringing about higher GDP growth.   However, should a protracted period of political uncertainty (extending to the conduct of economic policy) ensue, foreign investors may shun Georgia for a longer period.

36.   Continuing structural reforms will be key to strengthening Georgia's resilience to shocks, sustaining growth, attracting investment into export activities, and improving productivity; in short, in developing an enabling environment for export diversification in terms of both composition and direction.

I.   ECONOMIC ENVIRONMENT

(1)   INTRODUCTION

1.   Georgia, a small, strategically located middle-income country in the South Caucasus, has a population of 4.5 million and a natural resource base that offers strong economic growth potential. In Soviet times, Georgia exported agricultural and energy–intensive industrial products to the Soviet Union and was a popular tourist destination for the region. After independence in 1991, the economy collapsed under the impact of civil war and the loss of preferential access to Former Soviet Union (FSU) markets; output fell by 70% and exports by 90%, the worst decline suffered by any transition economy with sustained growth only resuming in 2003.[1]

2.   In 2008, Georgia had an estimated per capita income of US$2,900, over three times its level at the beginning of the review period in 2003. During most of this period, economic performance was impressive. Driven by rapidly rising foreign direct investment flows, annual economic growth averaged between 9% and 10% from 2003 to mid-2008. With the Georgian economy on a strong growth track for most of the review period, rising public expenditures, financed by a substantial increase in the tax to GDP ratio, were being directed at improvements in education and health services and in targeted social assistance for the poor as well as infrastructure.

3.   In 2008, the economy was hit by the twin shocks of the brief but disastrous armed conflict[2] with the Russian Federation in August and the global financial crisis in September, which brought about a reduction in FDI and workers' remittances, a collapse in export demand, and a sharp contraction in bank lending. Damage to infrastructure, caused by the conflict, as well as disruption to activity in several sectors – including construction, trade, and tourism – severely dampened growth. With the sudden deceleration in capital inflows and the onset of a credit drought, the economy contracted in the second half of the year with GDP growth for the full year of only 2.1%, the weakest result since 2000.

4.   Economic policies have been guided by reliance on the private sector for growth in a liberalized trade, investment, and business environment, and these policies have met with considerable success; the World Bank recognized Georgia as one of the world's fastest reforming economies. Georgia has implemented far-reaching structural reforms, aimed at developing a competitive private sector as the main engine of growth, but it has only partially succeeded in improving the productivity, and thus the external competitiveness, of the private sector. The rapid economic growth since 2003 has not been associated with growth of exports in GDP, its share remaining moderately low at about 20%, less than half the share of imports.

5.   Although there has been some diversification away from foodstuffs to high-technology products, Georgia's export structure remains quite concentrated in traditional sectors like base metals, minerals, and agriculture, whose productivity is relatively low. Continuing structural reforms will be key to strengthening Georgia's resilience to shocks, sustaining growth, attracting investment into export activities, and improving productivity: in short, in developing an enabling environment for export diversification in terms of both composition and direction.

---

[1] Asian Development Bank (2007), pp. 7-8.

[2] In December 2008 the EU Council established an Independent International Fact-Finding Mission on the Conflict in Georgia to investigate the origins and the course of the conflict in Georgia. In September 2009, the results of the investigation were presented in the form of a Report.

(2) MAIN FEATURES OF THE GEORGIAN ECONOMY

(i) 1991 to 2003: from independence to the Rose Revolution

6.   Georgia was among the first republics of the FSU to proclaim independence in 1991. During the four years of upheaval that followed, the country experienced civil unrest and internal conflicts, in particular the war in the Abkhazian region, which created serious refugee problems and closure of its trade routes. Prior to independence, the Georgian economy had been closely integrated with that of the Soviet Union with trade accounting for an estimated 40% of GDP, and nearly all exports directed to, and three quarters of imports coming from, the Soviet republics. The industrial sector accounted for about one third of the economy and although Georgia lacked cheap sources of energy, it produced steel pipes, locomotives, and other energy-intensive products for export. The competitiveness of Georgia's heavy industry was dependent on the supply of natural gas from Turkmenistan at artificially low prices and on inflated prices for final products.

7.   The dissolution of the FSU had serious effects on the Georgian economy: the price of gas and oil rose dramatically in the early 1990s, making Georgia's heavy industry uncompetitive and halting production in Georgia's industrial centres. In addition, Russia's economic problems led to a collapse of demand for Georgia's agricultural goods (in which it had comparative advantage), and tourism, formerly an important source of income, virtually disappeared. Thus, like other CIS countries, Georgia had thousands of unemployed engineers and scientists but no industry that could employ them. In response, large numbers of skilled people withdrew from the market, many becoming attached to low productivity activities in agricultural and rural areas, some resorted to the public sector, and others migrated abroad. By 1994, Georgia's GDP was estimated at 17% of its 1990 level - the greatest fall among the countries of the FSU. Robust and sustained growth resumed in 2003 but the level of output in 2007 was still only an estimated 70% of the 1990 level, in stark contrast to the performance of most of the CIS countries.[3]

8.   Despite the problems, the overriding objective of Georgia's economic policies during the 1990s was to create and develop a market economy through privatization of state-owned commercial enterprises, deregulation of prices, and liberalization of its trade and investment regimes. This included in particular: the establishment of a legislative basis for economic reform; the creation of an independent monetary and credit system; the introduction of a national currency; and the complete liberalization of prices, which entailed removing from State regulation more than 90% of the retail prices of consumer goods and services and 95% of the prices of industrial goods. Additional government resolutions substantially removed all energy, transport, and other public utility prices from State administration, replacing control with tariff regulation either by local governments or, in the cases of electricity and natural gas, by independent departments set up for this purpose. The Government rescinded exclusive rights granted to certain economic agents, abolished restrictions on competition in certain activities, and cut subsidized credits to state-owned enterprises.   The Government also took substantial steps towards the transformation of property via mass privatization through which State enterprises began to be transformed into joint stock companies.

9.   After a brief period of stabilization in the late 1990s, Georgia lost its reform momentum as its governance capacity deteriorated and public trust in the Government dissipated. The Government became increasingly incapable of resisting pressure from vested interests, with negative consequences for the provision of basic public services. Following the Rose Revolution in November 2003, the policy environment was transformed, with the new administration demonstrating a strong political will to carry through reforms on several fronts: effective anticorruption measures,

---

[3] World Bank (2009b), p. 15.

strong macroeconomic management, and follow-through on structural and selected sector reforms. However, growth has not been accompanied by net job creation, and unemployment is on the rise, topping 16% in 2008 and contributing to the persistence of poverty.

10.   In terms of foreign trade, the state-planning system with its preponderance of bilateral countertrade agreements was brought to an end. Much of the transformation to a market economy had been achieved by the time of Georgia's accession to the WTO in 2000 and, broadly speaking, trade and trade-related policies pursued during the review period have built on those achievements. Partly with a view to eventual membership of the EU[4], the Government has focused on harmonizing Georgia's legal system to international norms, by introducing or amending legislation in key trade-related areas such as customs; banking and other services; intellectual property; standardization and certification; government procurement; privatization; competition; and business legislation.

(ii)   Structure of the economy

11.   Fertile land and a favourable climate enable diverse agricultural production, including a range of fruits and vegetables, livestock, dairy products, nuts, and tea. The country has a long history of viticulture and some 500 varieties of grapes are cultivated. Recent investments in oil exploration have indicated oil and gas potential. Other physical resources include manganese, iron, coal, copper, gold, granite, limestone, marble, and mineral waters. Dense forests cover one third of the country and numerous fast-lowing rivers offer good hydropower potential although the country imports the bulk of its energy needs, including natural gas and oil. Its location on the "Silk Road" between Europe and Asia makes it a transit conduit for goods being shipped through the Caucasus.

12.   Georgia's economy has undergone significant structural change since independence. Around 15 years ago, shares of agriculture, industry, and services in GDP were more or less evenly split. The share of agriculture has since declined significantly and stood at an estimated 10.3% of GDP in 2008 (Table I.1) although the sector remains critical for the Georgian economy. Over 53% of the labour force (including wage labour and the self-employed) depend on agriculture for their livelihood and agriculture accounts for 18% of exports although Georgia's net trade in agriculture and food products remains negative.

Table I.1
Basic economic indicators, 2002-08

	2002	2003	2004	2005	2006	2007	2008
Real GDP at 2003 market prices (lari million)	..	8,564.1	9,065.9	9,935.6	10,868.0	12,208.8	12,460.7
Real GDP at 2003 market price (US$ million)	..	3,990.8	4,729.1	5,481.2	6,117.1	7,307.8	8,362.0
Current GDP at factor prices (lari million)	6,960.7	8,041.9	8,989.6	10,284.5	12,046.9	14,611.1	16,516.6
Current GDP at market prices (lari million)	7,456.0	8,564.1	9,824.3	11,621.0	13,789.9	16,993.8	19,069.6
Current GDP at market prices (US$ million)	3,398.1	3,990.8	5,124.7	6,411.0	7,761.7	10,171.9	12,797.0
GDP per capita at current market price (lari)	1,705.6	1,972.1	2,276.7	2,689.1	3,133.1	3,866.9	4,351.7
GDP per capita at current market price (US$)	777.3	919.0	1,187.6	1,483.5	1,763.6	2,314.6	2,920.3
GDP by economic activity at constant prices (annual %age change)							
Agriculture, forestry and fishing	-1.4	10.3	-7.9	12.0	-11.7	3.3	-2.1
Mining and quarrying	29.8	-2.1	-19.9	-7.8	18.7	19.9	17.0
Manufacturing	13.1	7.9	7.2	13.6	16.5	15.9	-2.1

Table I.1 (cont'd)

---

[4] On 1 December 2009, the *Treaty of Lisbon amending the Treaty on European Union and the Treaty establishing the European Community* (done at Lisbon, 13 December 2007) entered into force. On 29 November 2009, the WTO received a Verbal Note (WT/L/779) from the Council of the European Union and the Commission of the European Communities stating that, by virtue of the *Treaty of Lisbon*, as of 1 December 2009, the European Union replaces and succeeds the European Community.

	2002	2003	2004	2005	2006	2007	2008
Electricity, gas and water	-10.2	9.2	-4.0	5.1	13.4	6.8	-2.7
Construction	43.1	46.6	35.9	14.1	8.5	14.6	-11.0
Services	5.4	10.5	7.5	10.4	14.6	12.1	4.6
Trade and repair	3.9	12.1	8.2	9.4	19.7	9.6	10.4
Restaurant and hotels	7.6	14.2	3.5	16.6	10.5	11.4	5.0
Transport, storage and communication	8.7	8.4	7.1	10.9	15.7	10.9	-2.4
Financial intermediation	22.9	18.1	12.8	52.8	36.9	15.3	3.3
Real estate, renting and business activities	-1.9	10.6	11.8	5.4	8.6	14.7	2.2
Public administration and defence	1.2	-2.3	9.7	-6.3	-2.4	15.9	10.3
Education	1.5	1.5	1.8	13.8	12.1	9.5	13.7
Health and social work	6.5	1.7	4.2	7.6	15.4	10.4	5.9
Other	3.7	18.6	7.0	16.8	7.1	23.5	-0.1
Share of main sector in current GDP, factor prices (%)							
Agriculture, forestry and fishing	20.6	20.6	17.9	16.7	12.8	10.7	10.3
Mining and quarrying	0.7	0.9	0.9	0.9	1.2	1.0	0.8
Manufacturing	13.7	13.9	13.4	13.7	12.7	12.7	12.3
Electricity, gas and water	4.5	4.0	3.4	3.2	3.1	2.8	2.5
Construction	5.5	6.8	8.8	9.1	7.9	7.8	6.1
Services	56.1	54.8	56.5	57.7	63.2	66.1	69.3
Trade and repair	13.7	14.1	13.9	13.5	15.6	14.8	16.1
Restaurant and hotels	3.1	3.0	3.0	3.2	2.6	2.4	2.4
Transport, storage and communication	15.2	14.8	14.6	14.0	13.2	12.1	11.6
Financial intermediation	1.6	1.6	1.4	2.3	2.4	2.5	2.4
Real estate, renting and business activities	6.4	6.4	6.3	6.0	6.5	6.5	6.6
Public administration and defence	4.2	3.8	6.4	7.3	9.7	14.9	17.3
Education	3.9	3.5	3.8	3.7	4.2	3.8	4.0
Health and social work	5.0	4.3	3.8	3.9	5.0	4.7	4.7
Other	2.9	3.2	3.2	3.7	3.8	4.4	4.3
Less: FISIM adjustment[a]	1.0	1.0	0.8	1.3	0.9	1.1	1.3
Share of sector in total employment (%)							
Agriculture, forestry and fishing	53.8	54.9	54.0	54.3	55.3	53.4	..
Mining and quarrying	0.3	0.2	0.2	0.3	0.2	0.3	..
Manufacturing	4.6	4.9	5.1	5.1	4.7	4.9	..
Electricity, gas and water	1.4	1.1	1.2	1.3	1.1	1.1	..
Construction	1.9	2.2	2.4	2.5	3.1	4.2	..
Services	37.9	36.6	37.2	36.4	35.7	36.3	..
Trade and utilities	11.7	10.9	11.0	10.8	9.6	9.9	..
Restaurant and hotels	0.8	0.9	1.1	0.9	1.0	1.1	..
Transport, storage and communication	4.3	4.2	4.2	4.0	4.5	4.2	..
Financial intermediation	0.4	0.5	0.7	0.8	0.8	1.0	..
Real estate, renting and business activities	1.1	1.8	1.6	1.5	1.5	2.0	..
Public administration	5.9	5.0	4.9	4.7	4.5	3.8	..
Education	7.1	7.5	7.5	7.5	7.6	7.3	..
Health and social work	3.4	2.7	3.1	3.3	3.0	3.5	..
Other	3.2	3.1	3.1	2.9	3.2	3.5	..

..   Not available.

a   FISIM stands for Financial Intermediation Services Indirectly Measured.

Source: Georgia Statistics online information. Viewed at: http://www.statistics.ge/main.php?pform=54&plang=1 [May 2009].

13.   Labour productivity in agriculture is barely one-tenth of that in the rest of the economy, generating relatively low incomes and thus poverty. According to the latest poverty assessment of Georgia by the World Bank, rural areas account for 59% of the total poor and 62% of the extreme poor in the country.[5] With a widening rural-urban income gap, agriculture's performance is critical for poverty reduction, which continues to be prevalent in rural areas left behind by the economic growth of recent years. To reduce poverty in the longer term, the World Bank recommends the introduction of measures to revitalize the agriculture sector, where livelihoods continue to rely on low-productivity subsistence agriculture.

14.   Industry – comprising mining, manufacturing, utilities and construction – contributed 21.7% of GDP in 2008 and provided employment to 10.5% of the total employed labour force in 2007, making labour productivity more than twice the level in the rest of the economy. The most significant parts of the sector are the agri-processing and energy industries. Construction work on two international pipelines contributed to significant expansion in the construction, industrial, and services sectors in the early 2000s.

15.   The services sector, particularly market-oriented services, has undergone rather rapid development, in particular with regard to trade, transport, and financial services, as well as public administration and defence. It accounted for over 69% of GDP in 2008, up from 56% in 2002, engaging over one third the employed labour force in 2008. Transport is a key sector given Georgia's location as the shortest transit link from Azerbaijan and Central Asia to Europe.

(iii)   The shadow economy

16.   Studies carried out over the past few years suggest that Georgia had one of the largest shadow economies in the former Soviet Union; some estimates indicate that it was as much as 67% of GDP in 2000.[6] The size of informal sector production and household production for own final use is likely to have declined since the present Government came to power in late 2003.[7] Reform measures and the targeting of several high-profile businessmen on charges of corruption and tax evasion may have spurred enterprises to start paying taxes and enter the formal economy. The authorities maintain that although there are no official estimates of the current size of the shadow economy it has declined significantly, as witnessed for example by the increase in the number of registered enterprises (from 36,000 in 2005 to 51,000 in 2007) and the rise in the tax to GDP ratio from 18% in 2004 to 25% by 2007.

(3)   MAIN ECONOMIC DEVELOPMENTS

(i)   Macroeconomic performance

17.   Prior to the August 2008 armed conflict with Russia, the Georgian economy was growing strongly, with GDP rising by nearly 10% per annum on average led by construction, financial intermediation, communications and, more recently, manufacturing. Underlying this was a rapidly improving business climate and increasing inflows of foreign direct investment, which jumped from 8.4% of GDP in 2003 to an estimated 17.2% in 2007. Rising public expenditures, financed by a substantial increase in the tax to GDP ratio were being directed at improvements in education and

---

[5] World Bank (2009b), p. 52.

[6] Based on Schneider and Enste (2002). The figure is quoted in OECD (2009).

[7] Informal sector production is defined in the OECD paper as low-level production with the intent of generating employment and income to the persons concerned. This is quite different from underground production, i.e. activities that are deliberately concealed from public authorities to avoid taxes, social security payments or certain legal/administrative standards.

health services and in targeted social assistance for the poor as well as infrastructure (Table I.2). Economic policies were guided overall by reliance on the private sector for growth in a liberalized trade, investment, and business environment.

Table I.2
Selected macroeconomic indicators, 2002-08

	2002	2003	2004	2005	2006	2007	2008
National accounts				(Percentage change)			
Real GDP (at 2003 prices)	5.5	11.1	5.9	9.6	9.4	12.3	2.1
XGS/GDP (%) (at current market price)	29.2	31.8	31.6	33.7	32.9	31.2	28.7
MGS/GDP (%) (at current market price)	42.4	46.4	48.2	51.6	57.0	58.0	57.7
Unemployment rate (%)	12.6	11.5	12.6	13.8	13.6	13.3	16.5
Prices and interest rates				(Per cent)			
Inflation (CPI, %age change, period average)	5.6	4.8	5.7	8.2	9.2	9.2	10.0
Inflation (CPI, %age change, end period)	5.4	7.0	7.6	6.2	8.8	11.0	5.5
Deposit rate[a]	9.82	9.28	7.24	7.55	11.44	9.52	10.39
	(10.23)	(9.19)	(7.66)	(5.94)	(6.60)	(7.28)	(9.01)
Lending rate[a]	31.83	32.27	31.23	21.63	18.75	20.41	21.24
	(29.27)	(27.62)	(27.06)	(24.18)	(22.50)	(18.64)	(20.43)
Money credit (end period)				(Percentage change)			
Reserve money (M1)	19.7	14.3	46.9	16.2	26.3	40.1	-7.8
Broad money[b]	17.9	22.8	42.4	26.5	39.7	49.7	6.9
Credit to private sector	21.4	23.5	29.1	78.3	56.7	79.1	31.7
Exchange rate							
Lari/US$ (annual average)	2.19	2.15	1.92	1.81	1.78	1.67	1.49
Real effective exchange rate (%age change)	-6.4	-6.8	6.8	6.3	5.9	3.8	16.4
Nominal effective exchange rate (%age change)	-3.3	-4.9	6.4	3.7	1.9	0.1	13.4
			(Per cent of GDP, unless otherwise indicated)				
Consolidated Government operations							
Revenue and grants	..	15.7	23.1	24.3	27.9	29.3	30.7
Tax revenue	..	11.7	15.6	17.1	19.2	21.6	24.9
Current expenditure	..	14.7	18.7	20.9	21.6	25.8	28.4
Operational balance	..	1.0	4.4	3.5	6.3	3.5	2.3
Capital spending and net lending	..	..	2.0	5.1	9.3	8.2	8.7
Total balance	..	..	2.4	-1.6	-3.0	-4.7	-6.4
Government total debt (end-period)	..	53.8	43.8	35.1	28.0	23.1	27.0
Domestic debt	..	18.3	16.0	13.2	11.0	8.8	7.7
Saving and investment							
Gross national savings	19.8	23.2	22.5	22.8	14.9	14.6	8.5
Gross domestic investment	28.5	31.3	31.9	33.5	30.9	32.1	27.0
Savings-investment gap	-8.7	-8.1	-9.4	-10.7	-16.0	-17.5	-18.5
External sector							
Current account balance	-6.3	-9.6	-6.9	-11.1	-15.1	-19.8	-22.8
Net merchandise trade	-14.4	-16.0	-17.9	-18.9	-26.0	-28.5	-30.0
Merchandise exports	17.8	20.8	21.3	23.0	21.5	20.5	19.0
Merchandise imports	32.1	36.8	39.2	41.9	47.5	49.0	48.9
Services balance	1.3	1.5	1.4	1.3	2.0	1.6	0.2
Capital account	0.5	0.5	0.8	0.9	2.2	1.3	0.8

Table I.2 (cont'd)

	2002	2003	2004	2005	2006	2007	2008
Financial account	6.4	8.8	9.4	11.5	19.4	22.5	23.4
Foreign direct investment in Georgia	4.7	8.4	9.6	7.1	15.1	17.2	12.2
Balance-of-payments	0.9	-0.5	3.5	1.7	5.7	3.7	1.0
Merchandise exports (%age change)	21.6	37.7	31.5	34.8	13.2	25.3	16.3
Merchandise imports (%age change)	4.5	34.4	36.7	33.8	37.2	35.2	25.6
Service exports (%age change)	30.0	12.1	21.1	28.9	23.8	23.6	15.2
Service imports (%age change)	53.4	9.2	22.3	30.2	15.1	28.3	32.7
Foreign exchange reserves[c] (US$ million, end-period)	199.3	191.3	375.4	477.6	929.9	1,346.3	1,467.8
In months of imports of goods and services	1.6	1.2	1.8	1.7	2.5	2.7	..
External debt (US$ million)	1,858.8	2,042.1	2,138.0	2,095.0	2,328.0	3,136.0	4,581.0
Debt service ratio[d]	..	..	41.7	32.7	30.0	30.7	35.6

..   Not available.

a   Data in brackets refers to interest rates in foreign currencies.

b   Broad money consists of cash outside banks (except reserves in vaults of commercial banks) and total national currency deposits with commercial banks, including foreign currency denominated deposits.

c   Excluding gold, Special Drawing Rights, and Reserve Position in the IMF.

d   Debt service in per cent of exports of goods and services.

Source: Georgia Statistics online information. Viewed at: http://www.statistics.ge/main.php?plang=1 [June 2009]; IMF (2009), *International Financial Statistics*, June; National Bank of Georgia online information. Viewed at: http://www.nbg.gov.ge/index.php?m=306 [June 2006]; and data provided by the authorities.

18.   However, the recent growth has largely been jobless in net terms, as high quality private-sector jobs created have just about compensated for job cuts resulting from public sector reforms. The total number of active persons in the labour force has been declining, from 2.1 million in 2002 to 1.9 million in 2008. Over the same period, the unemployment rate rose from 12.6% in 2002 to 16.5% in 2008, with significant lay-offs reported recently in the construction, financial and retail sectors. Poverty remains widespread at an estimated 22.1% in 2008 compared with 21.3% in 2007[8], an increase probably due to the conflict and the economic downturn.

19.   The August 2008 armed conflict with Russia took a significant toll on the country, with about 127,500 people displaced, much physical capital destroyed, important trade routes disrupted, and the Government's authority in large segments of its territory undermined as 20% of Georgian territory was occupied by Russia.[9] The armed conflict resulted in severe shocks to macroeconomic stability and a sharp deterioration in investor and consumer confidence. GDP growth declined sharply in the second half of 2008, resulting in real growth of 2.1% for the year as a whole, down from over 12% in 2007. In the first quarter of 2009, the economy contracted by 5.9%. The on-going global economic crisis continues to cast a shadow over Georgia's growth prospects with lower commodity prices (in particular for fertilizers and metals), a drop in demand for Georgian exports and a significant decline in private capital inflows, which have been the main driver of growth, all negatively affecting the economy.

---

[8] Estimates provided by the Ministry of Economic Development, according to which the subsistence minimum was GEL 127.9 per month in 2008, a 52% increase compared with 2004 when poverty was an estimated 24.6%.

[9] According to a recent UN/World Bank report, about 106,000 of the displaced persons have returned to the Shida Kartli region in the Gori Valley and have received assistance in the rehabilitation of damaged and destroyed houses. See UN and World Bank (2009), p. 8.

20.   Georgia has run a large current account deficit, which reflects high gross domestic investment (equal to 27% of GDP in 2008) in relation to national savings (8.5% of GDP in the same year).[10] The deficit has been expanding progressively both in absolute value terms and as a percentage of GDP since 2004 when it was 6.9%; in 2006 the overall deficit expanded to 15.1% of GDP, and widened further to 22.8% in 2008. While narrowing, the current account deficit remained high at 17.6% of GDP for the first quarter of 2009. The marked deterioration in 2006-07 was attributable to a sharp widening of the trade deficit, mainly the result of the Russian trade embargo, which undermined Georgian exports. Overall, current account developments have been dominated by rapid import growth, due to growing domestic demand, FDI-related imports, and rising energy prices. The current account deficit has been covered by the surpluses in the capital and financial accounts, mainly due to large FDI inflows, which increased significantly between 2003 and mid-2008. The surplus on the capital and financial account helped to improve the official reserves position, which was at around US$1.5 billion (about 3 months of import cover) at end 2008, a significant improvement over 2003 when it was as low as 1.2 months of import cover.

21.   According to the IMF, the external current account deficit narrowed substantially during the second half of 2008 (by around 4% of GDP) led by large official inflows from September.[11] The deficit is narrowing faster than expected, led by declining imports; declining import demand, and improved confidence, which have reduced pressures on the exchange rate. The trade balance remained broadly unchanged relative to the first half of the year as a severe drop in metal prices and exports was broadly offset by lower FDI-related imports and petroleum prices. Private capital inflows, which have been financing the current account deficit, dropped from US$1.7 billion during the first half of the year to an estimated US$450 million during the second half.

22.   Improving productivity and thus the external competitiveness of the private sector is of particular importance in generating sustained growth and improving the current account balance. The key to raising productivity and competitiveness is continued efforts to improve infrastructure and the business environment. However, rapid economic growth during the period (driven primarily by construction, telecommunications, finance, and other services) has not been associated with rapid growth of exports relative to the overall economy: merchandise exports as a share of GDP remained relatively low and stable at about 20%.

(ii)   Monetary and exchange rate policies

23.   The IMF characterizes the exchange rate regime as "managed floating" with no predetermined path for the exchange rate. The authorities believe a managed floating exchange rate regime remains appropriate for Georgia, with the National Bank of Georgia (NBG) acting to limit nominal appreciation. The August conflict led to pressure on the currency and a loss of international reserves but gross reserves were US$1.5 billion by the end of June 2009, re-establishing the level observed before the August conflict. The currency was devalued by about 16% in November 2008 and currency auctions were introduced in March 2009 to allow the market to determine appropriate levels. Exchange rates have been relatively stable in 2009, aided by the reduction in demand for foreign exchange due to slowing import demand.

24.   Inflation was maintained in single digits through most of the review period but crept into double digits late in 2007 largely due to rising energy and food prices, as well as large capital inflows.

---

[10] Whether Georgia's large current account deficit is sustainable raises the question of the potential risk of the widening of the savings-investment gap, stemming from the expected slowdown in FDI from its recent high levels. A slowdown will require an adjustment in the savings-investment gap, either through a retrenchment in investment or through higher private savings to finance growing domestic private investment.

[11] IMF (2009a), p. 6.

Inflation slowed considerably in 2008 as global commodity prices receded and domestic demand contracted given the NBG's focus on tightening monetary policy to contain inflation pressures in the first half of 2008. End-period inflation was 5.5% for 2008 and, according to the authorities, 12-month inflation was only 2.3% as of end-June 2009. In the second half of 2008, the NBG changed focus and deployed monetary instruments as part of the macroeconomic stimulus package. To provide needed liquidity, reserve requirements were lifted although the desired response from the banks – in terms of supplying credit to the private sector at affordable rates – has been disappointing temporarily.[12]

(iii) Fiscal policy

25.   From 2004 to mid 2008, the key improvements in tax revenue – a simplified and more transparent tax policy, a reduction in the number of taxes, efficient and corruption-free tax administration, expanding economic activity, and the increase in taxes collected on imports, reflecting strong import growth – pushed revenue collection to new heights and helped to create the fiscal space for growth-oriented public spending. During this period, trade taxes, comprising customs and excise duties and VAT, increased as a share of total tax revenues from 32% to 38% although customs duties declined markedly in line with recent tariff liberalization, accounting for only 3% of total trade taxes in 2008 compared with 16% in 2004. At the beginning of 2008, the authorities established a sovereign wealth fund to save resources generated by the revenue performance.

26.   The August conflict and the economic downturn led to revenue shortfalls compared with pre-crisis targets, in particular with respect to VAT revenues. Central to the authorities' fiscal response have been expenditure measures underwritten by significant donor inflows to support job-creating investment projects and the broadening of the social safety net. Although the fiscal deficit is expected to increase to around 9% in 2009, covered in large part by increased donor support, the Government is committed to reducing it to between 2% and 3% by 2013.[13]

27.   The major macroeconomic challenge in 2009 is to restore private capital inflows to support growth. The Government estimates that FDI inflows will be of the order of US$900 million, 40% lower than in 2008, which significantly reduces an important source of growth for the economy. The significant financial support made available to Georgia by the international community will be directed to capital expenditures necessitated by the conflict[14], as well as spending to establish a foundation for sustained economic growth over the medium-term.[15] These resources will help to support growth in 2009 but cannot be a full substitute for private-sector investment. To enhance

---

[12] The central bank raised the policy rate to 12% in April 2008, cut it in September, and by the end of the year it was at 8%.

[13] IMF (2009).

[14] The international community – through an October 2008 Donors' conference led by the World Bank and the European Commission – responded to the crisis by providing pledges of financial support totalling US$4.5 billion over 2008-10 in order to: provide financial assistance in light of the sudden decline in capital inflows; help Georgia with its external financing needs to maintain its macroeconomic stability; and assist with the rebuilding of its damaged infrastructure and help Georgia cope with the downturn of the economy and the substantial social needs of its (new and past) displaced population. With donor money flowing in, the authorities have the room to expand fiscal policies further to counteract the adverse impact from the shocks on economic activity. The 2009 fiscal deficit is expected to increase to 6.8% of GDP, up from 6% in 2008. The authorities have committed to allocate donor assistance in a fully transparent and efficient manner.

[15] According to the authorities, in 2009 fiscal policies will support the economic recovery with a stimulus package that includes a moderate increase in total spending, a reduction in the rate of the profit tax, and a shift from import-intensive defence spending to labour-intensive construction projects. Particular emphasis will be given to capital projects to improve medium-term competitiveness as the basis for future growth. These projects will be financed mainly from the pledges of the international community.

Georgia's appeal to investors, the authorities consider that maintaining macroeconomic stability and intensifying economic reforms are essential elements in moving forward.

28.   Although Georgia is likely to require significant external financing during 2008-11, its external debt is expected to remain sustainable in the medium term. As a result of appropriate debt management and effective macroeconomic policies, Georgia had a low level of indebtedness prior to the economic downturn, with external public debt declining from 44.9% in 2003 to 22% in 2006, and a record low of 17.6% in 2007. Following the armed conflict, external public debt rose in 2008 but remained manageable at 21.7% of GDP.

(iv)   Structural reforms and private-sector development

29.   Since 2004, Georgia has implemented a policy of wide-ranging economic reform to foster economic growth through private-sector investment. Georgia eliminated barriers to private-sector activity by deregulating the economy, privatizing most state assets, simplifying and reducing the number of taxes leading to a higher tax to GDP ratio, liberalizing the trade regime, investing in infrastructure, and significantly reducing bureaucratic barriers. This has helped to increase transparency and thus accountability and thereby reduce discretion and corruption.

(a)   Improving the business environment

30.   The Government has remained committed to its medium-term reform agenda, continuing improvement of the business environment through reducing tax rates on income and simplifying tax administration, significantly improving customs services, and rationalizing the licensing system. The latter was a key area in transforming the business environment. Consequently, the cost of doing business has fallen appreciably and inward FDI has surged. Arbitrary tax enforcement, inadequate legal protection, discretionary application of laws and regulations, and pervasive corruption were among the main reasons why foreign investors previously shunned Georgia.

31.   Georgia is ranked 11th out of 183 economies in the World Bank's *Doing Business* index for 2010[16], and has been among the top ten reforming countries for the last four years. When Georgia began major reforms in 2005, it was ranked behind many of the countries in the region, such as Armenia, Russia, Kazakhstan, Turkey; it has moved up 101 positions since then (Table I.3). According to the World Bank's index, reforms in Georgia have made it easier to start a business, have cut the number of activities that require licences from 950 to 150, eased the cost of separating redundant workers, and cut the time and cost to register property. However, attention is still needed in some areas, such as further simplifying tax collection and enhancing investor protection.

32.   Despite a number of successful reforms, weaknesses remain: the most recent World Economic Forum Global Competitiveness Index[17] ranks Georgia 90th out of 134 countries. The report highlights Georgia's reduced regulatory burden and labour market efficiency as sources of competitive advantage but also lists a large number of sources of competitive disadvantage, including: lack of higher education and training, financing constraints particularly for small enterprises, limited financial market sophistication, small market size, and deficiencies regarding availability of technology, poor business sophistication, and very limited innovation and R&D capacity.[18]

---

[16] World Bank (2009a). The report covers June 2008 to May 2009.

[17] World Economic Forum (2008).

[18] Rapid economic growth requires *inter alia* public policies that foster education and training as well as a research and innovation policy directly relevant to a country's sustainable economic policy objectives. See Gylfason and Hochreiter (2008); and Ivianiashvili-Orbeliani (2009).

Table I.3
Ease of doing business, 2005 and 2010

Ease of ...	Doing business 2010 rank	Doing business 2005 rank[a]	Change in rank
Doing business	11	112	+101
Starting a business	5	59	+54
Dealing with licences/permits	7	152	+145
Employing workers	9	71	+62
Registering property	2	18	+16
Getting credit	30	96	+66
Protecting investors	41	133	+92
Paying taxes	64	160	+96
Trading across borders	30	149	+119
Enforcing contracts	41	56	+15
Closing a business	95	98	+3

a   Out of 181 economies.

Source: World Bank (2009), *Doing Business in Georgia 2010.*   Viewed at: http://www.doingbusiness.org/economy rankings/.

(b)   Tax and customs reforms

33.   The Government has adopted a new tax regime that has (i) simplified the Tax Code and substantially reduced the tax burden on firms and individuals by reducing the number of taxes, (ii) abolished exemptions and broadened the tax base, (iii) lowered some rates to facilitate compliance, and (iv) distributed the tax burden more equitably. Georgia opted for a flat-rate personal income tax in 2004 to reduce tax evasion and to increase the incentive for economic activity in the formal sector (Table I.4). The profit tax is also levied at a flat rate and was brought down from 20% to 15% in 2008; and the VAT single rate was reduced from 20% to 18% in 2006. As a result of these reforms, tax revenues increased from 18% of GDP in 2004 to 22% in 2006 and 25% in 2007. Institutional reforms in tax administration and stricter enforcement of tax laws have also helped. Non-tax revenues grew by 52% in 2006, mainly due to higher collections from license and permit fees, state duties, fines, and penalties.

Table I.4
Main taxes and tax rates, 2005-08
(Per cent)

Type of taxes	Before 2005	2005-07	2008
Income tax	12-20	12	25 (unified with social tax in 2008 with stepwise reduction to 15% by 2011)
Social tax	27-33	20	Abolished (merged with personal income tax)
Corporate (profit) tax	20	20	15
Value-added tax	20	18	18
Customs duty	0-30	0, 5, 12	0, 5, 12

Source: Asian Development Bank (2007), *Country Economic Report: Georgia*, Appendix 3, p. 24, June. Viewed at: http://www.adb.org/Documents/CERs/GEO/CER-GEO-2007.pdf.

34.   The Government adopted a new Customs Code in 2006, which simplified customs requirements and reorganized the Customs Department. A law on customs tariffs abolished the import tariff on most items (the laws later moved to the tax code); on other items the simple unweighted import tariff fell from 7.4% in 2004 to 1.4% in 2007. As a result of these and related

reforms, Georgia has a more open trade regime. The reforms have reduced economic distortions and the scope for corruption, and customs and border processing time for businesses.

(c)   Privatization

35.   The Government of Georgia has privatized most of the largest formerly state-owned enterprises.[19] Georgia intends to continue its policy of privatizing state-owned assets, including privatizing at least two thirds of the shares of the Georgian State Electricity Company; at least 24% of Poti Sea Port; Georgian Post; about 100,000 hectares of agricultural land; several regional airports; and numerous other state-owned enterprises. Privatization has played a role in attracting FDI, as the Government sold a wide variety of assets.

(4)   DEVELOPMENTS IN TRADE AND INVESTMENT

(i)   Merchandise trade

36.   The merchandise trade deficit nearly doubled during the review period, from 16% of GDP in 2003 to 30% by 2008.[20] This development has been largely conditioned by rapid import growth, due to growing domestic demand, FDI-related imports, and rising energy and commodity prices. According to the authorities, balance-of-payments data for the first half of 2009 show that exports and imports of goods declined by 35% and 38% respectively (compared with the first 6 months of 2008), which reflects a fall in commodity prices as well as reduced domestic demand.

(a)   Composition of trade

37.   Overall there has been a shift in export composition away from foodstuffs and agricultural products towards resource-based exports and, to some extent, high-technology products. However, although there has been some diversification, Georgia's export structure remains quite concentrated with the top five export categories – base metals, prepared foodstuffs, mineral products, chemical products, machinery and equipment, and cement – accounting for over 70% of export revenues. Metals including ferrous metals, copper, gold, and other minerals account for 20% of exports (Chart I.1 and Table AI.1). Exports of ferrous metals were buoyant in 2007, making up an increasing share of total exports, attributable to an increase in domestic production as well as rising steel prices. Overall, merchandise exports performed well in the first three-quarters of 2008 before weakening because of the global downturn. Export revenues for copper and other metals, among the country's top exports, were affected by the retreat in global demand and prices.

38.   Exports of cement rose sharply in 2007 and 2008, because of higher cement prices and the rehabilitation of Georgia's main cement-producing facilities. Car exports have risen in recent years, but these comprise re-exports to neighbouring countries; Azerbaijan absorbs much of the used cars imported into Georgia (mainly from Germany). Georgia remains largely dependent on exports of low-value-added goods, leaving it vulnerable to external shocks. The Russian embargo has had an impact on overall export revenue, although efforts to reorient domestic output to other markets have proved partially successful.

---

[19] See Ministry of Economic Development online information for a list of entities to be privatized. Viewed at: http://www.privatization.ge.

[20] The widening trade deficit has been partially offset by growing surpluses in other current account balances, including the non-factor services account, which has been boosted by revenues from oil pipeline services since the BTC pipeline has been running near full capacity.

Chart I.1
Product composition of merchandise trade, 2002 and 2008

Per cent

| 2002 | 2008 |

(a)   Exports (f.o.b.)

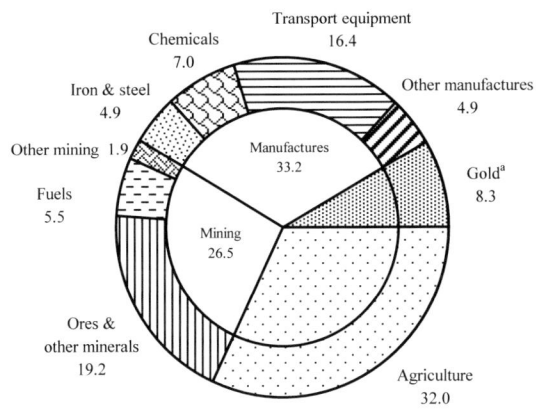

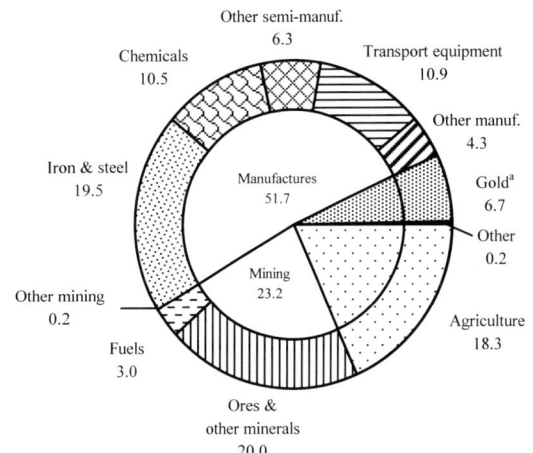

Total: US$346.3 million

Total: US$1,497.5 million

(b)   Imports (c.i.f.)

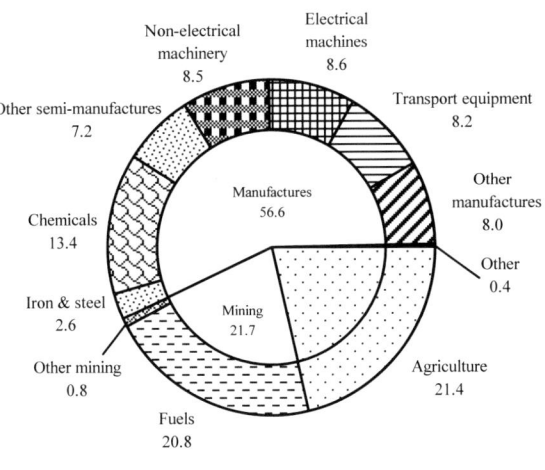

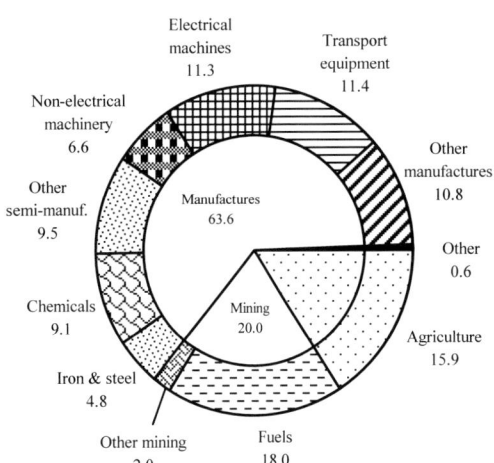

Total: US$793.3 million

Total: US$6,055.7 million

a   Non-monetary gold (excluding gold ores and concentrates).

Source: UNSD, Comtrade database (SITC Rev.3).

39.   Georgia's largest import category is hydrocarbons (mainly oil and gas). It continues to import electricity, but a large government programme is in place to revive and expand the considerable potential for hydroelectric power generation.[21] Georgia is a net exporter of electricity to Azerbaijan, Turkey, and Russia. Other major imports are motor cars, electronic and computer equipment, pharmaceuticals, and wheat (Table AI.2).

(b)   Direction of trade

40.   Georgia's trade with the CIS countries declined during the review period, with exports falling from nearly 49% in 2002 to 36% in 2008. Trade with Russia fell back sharply following the trade and transit embargo it imposed in 2006; until that point it had been Georgia's main trading partner (Chart I.2). While this contributed to a sharp slowdown in export growth, in particular in exports of alcoholic beverages, traditionally destined for Russia, other factors, including significant private capital inflows, cushioned the impact of the slowdown, allowing the Georgian economy to continue to grow.

41.   The EC27 is Georgia's main trade partner, accounting for roughly one fifth of exports and over one quarter of imports during the review period (Tables AI.3 and AI.4). Georgian exports were dominated by mineral fuels (around 40% of total exports) and agricultural products (almost 30%). Turkey has consolidated its position as Georgia's leading single trade partner, accounting for nearly 18% of exports and 15% of imports in 2008, following the decline of trade with Russia. Turkey absorbs the bulk of Georgia's exports of scrap metals. The United States became a leading destination for Georgian exports in 2007, buying up much of the output of ferrous alloys.

42.   In terms of imports, Turkey supplies mainly consumer goods and domestic appliances. Azerbaijan has become an important trading partner, providing a market for almost all of Georgia's cement production and is Georgia's main supplier of oil and gas. Ukraine supplies an assortment of goods, mainly consumer goods and metal products. Whereas Georgia was a net supplier of agricultural products in the FSU, it has become a net importer of agricultural and related products, which account for 15% of total imports.

(ii)   **Services trade**

43.   Services trade was roughly in balance during the review period, with exports and imports each amounting to about US$1.2 billion in 2008 (Chart I.3 and Table AI.5). Exports of travel, transportation, and other services remained quite constant in terms of trade shares over the review period, although in the transport sector Georgia has benefited from an increase in hydrocarbons transiting its territory, as oil and gas pipelines have become fully operational. On the import side, the share of travel has halved while the shares of transportation and financial and business services have increased.

---

[21] To this end, the Government sold several hydropower plants in 2007 to EnergoPro (Czech Republic), which pledged to invest heavily in the rehabilitation of the plants.

Chart I.2
Direction of merchandise trade, 2002 and 2008

Per cent

| 2002 | | 2008 |

(a)   Exports (f.o.b.)

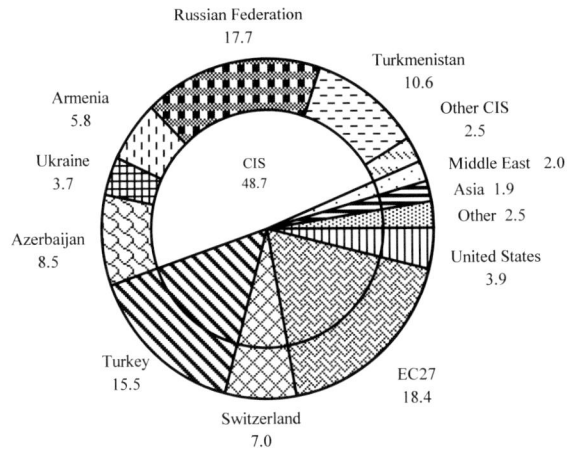
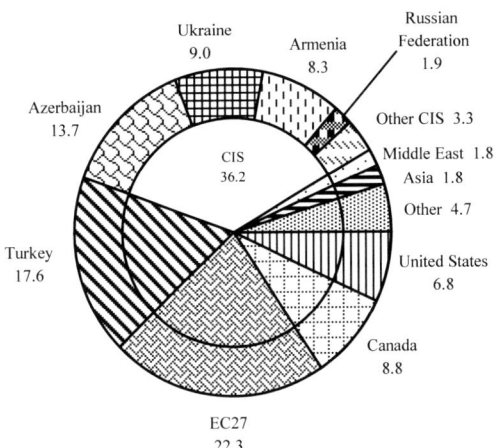

Total: US$346.3 million

Total: US$1,497.5 million

(b)   Imports (c.i.f.)

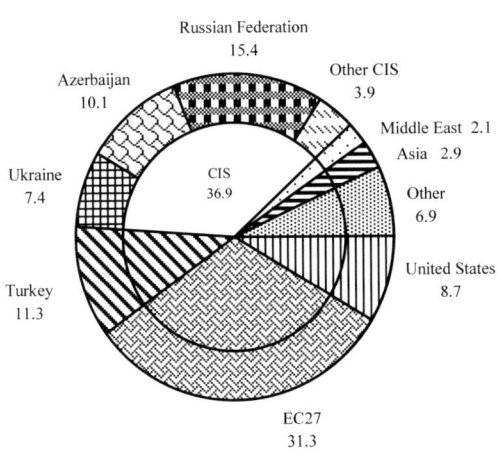
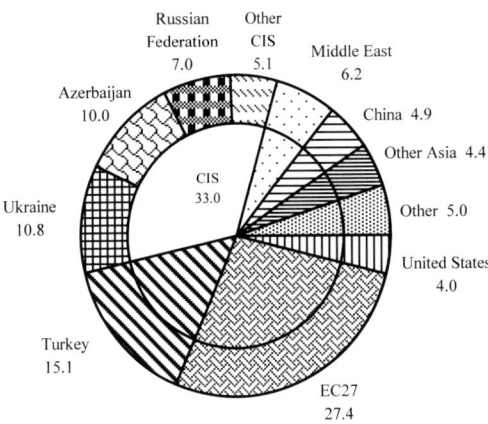

Total: US$793.3 million

Total: US$6,055.7 million

Source: UNSD, Comtrade database (SITC Rev.3).

Chart I.3
Trade in services, 2002 and 2008

Per cent

| 2002 | | 2008 |

(a) Exports

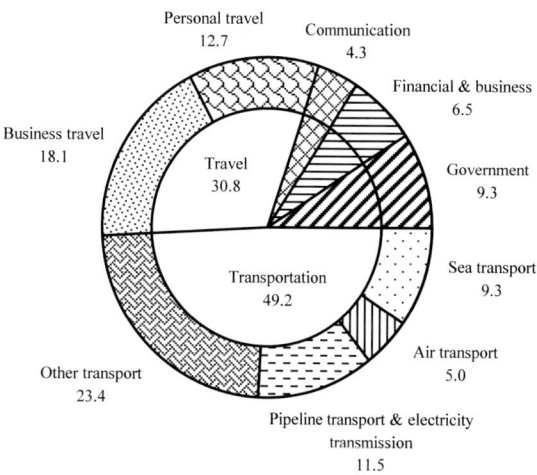

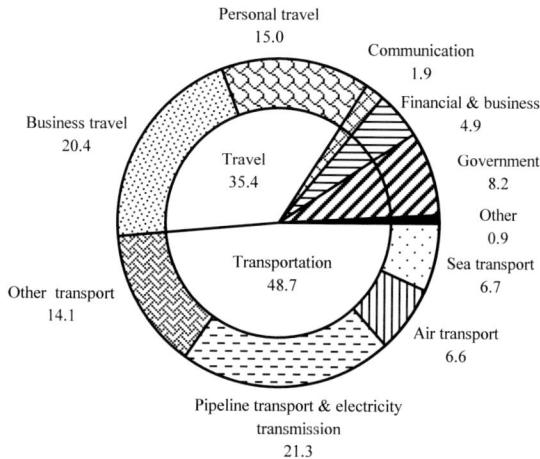

Total: US$408.4 million

Total: US$1,260.4 million

(b) Imports

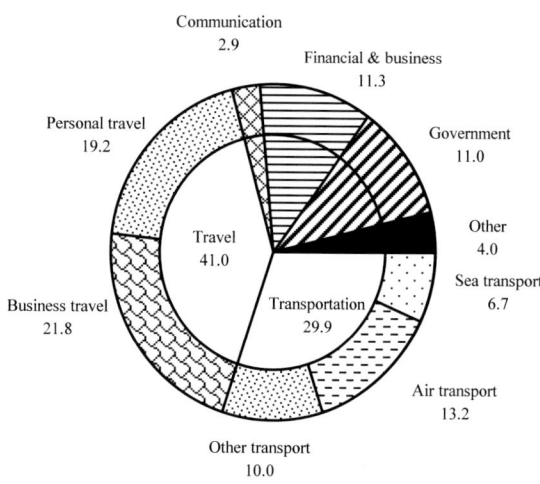

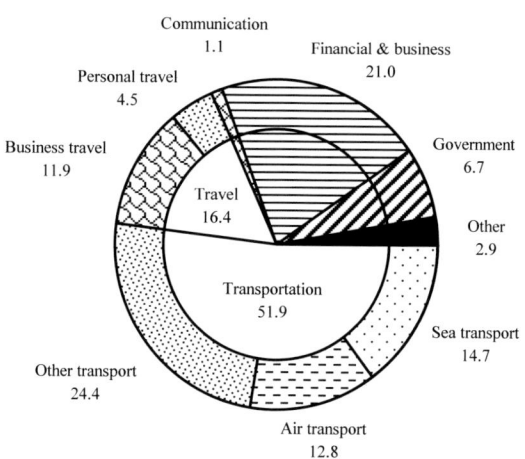

Total: US$363.4 million

Total: US$1,237.7 million

Source: National Bank of Georgia online information. Viewed at: http://www.nbg.gov.ge/index.php?m=
306&lng=eng#external [8 June 2009].

(iii)   **Trends in foreign direct investment (FDI)**

44.   During the review period, FDI responded to an improving business climate and aggressive privatization; it more than doubled between 2003 and 2007, from 8.4% of GDP to 17.2%. FDI inflows rose strongly in 2003-04 mainly due to the construction of the Baku-Tbilisi (BTC) oil pipeline and the South Caucasus gas pipeline (SCP). Since the completion of the BTC pipeline in 2004, the inflows have been largely non-pipeline related, from privatization in the network industries, real estate, basic industries, and mining and minerals processing (Table I.5). After declining in 2005, FDI increased in 2006 to nearly US$1.2 billion and to US$1.7 billion in 2007, as investment in manufacturing, banking and tourism compensated for lower pipeline-related investment. As a result of the August conflict, net foreign direct investment inflows fell in 2008 to around US$1.5 billion and the authorities forecast around US$900 million for 2009. In 2007, the EC27 accounted for over 56% of FDI inflows and in 2008 the EC, UAE, and Turkey accounted for nearly 60%.

Table I.5
Inflows of foreign direct investment, 2002-08
(US$ million and per cent)

	2002	2003	2004	2005	2006	2007	2008
Total inflows (US$ million)	160.2	334.6	492.3	452.8	1,170.1	1,750.2	1,564.0
% of GDP	4.7	8.4	9.6	7.1	15.1	17.2	12.2
				(Per cent of total)			
Inflows by origin							
EC27	34.9	28.2	39.2	54.2	34.2	56.2	30.5
United Kingdom	10.5	11.1	17.6	29.6	15.7	7.2	9.5
Netherlands	0.0	0.0	0.0	0.1	1.6	14.9	8.7
Austria	0.0	5.3	4.6	3.3	0.9	0.6	3.3
Germany	2.5	1.2	1.0	1.1	1.7	2.8	2.6
United Arab Emirates	0.0	0.1	0.0	0.1	0.0	6.5	19.6
United States	49.1	21.2	16.3	3.3	15.3	4.2	10.7
Turkey	5.3	5.1	6.8	4.8	10.9	4.7	10.5
British Virgin Islands	0.0	1.8	1.4	1.1	4.9	9.3	10.0
Switzerland	0.0	0.0	0.0	0.0	0.0	0.5	5.8
Kazakhstan	0.0	0.0	0.0	0.0	12.8	4.4	4.2
Belize	0.0	0.0	0.0	0.2	0.0	0.5	2.4
India	0.0	0.0	0.0	0.0	0.0	0.0	1.7
Russia	4.7	12.5	8.8	8.6	2.9	4.4	1.7
Azerbaijan	0.0	0.0	0.0	0.0	0.0	2.1	1.5
Japan	0.0	2.5	2.4	3.7	2.9	1.7	0.7
Bahamas	0.0	8.7	13.8	14.9	6.5	0.0	0.0
Other	6.0	19.8	11.3	9.1	9.5	7.5	2.1
Inflows by sector							
Agriculture	..	..	..	..	..	0.8	0.5
Industry	..	..	..	..	..	19.8	13.3
Energy sector	..	..	..	..	..	18.0	18.9
Construction	..	..	..	..	..	8.5	3.6
Transports and communications	..	..	..	..	..	20.7	27.0
Real estate	..	..	..	..	..	1.5	17.8
Other services	..	..	..	..	..	19.0	18.1
Banking system	..	..	..	..	..	6.8	0.5
Not stated[a]	..	..	..	..	..	4.9	0.3

..   Not available.

a   As a result of the privatization process, real estate bought by non-resident natural and legal persons is not defined yet.

Source: Data provided by the authorities; and Georgia Statistics online information. Viewed at: http://www.statistics.ge/main.php?plang=1 [June 2009].

45.   The majority of foreign (and local) investment has flowed into domestic infrastructure (transport, telecoms, energy, real estate) and domestic-oriented services (financial services, retail, construction, etc.). As investment has flowed into infrastructure, construction, and retail, domestic demand for construction materials, food, and consumer goods has boomed, but domestic production of these inputs has not kept pace. As there has been relatively limited investment in export-oriented agri-business and manufacturing, imports have soared, while exports have grown much more slowly. One of the aims of Georgia's investment policy is to persuade investors to set up production facilities in Georgia, either to serve the local market or to export. This is a challenge as investors need to be convinced not only that Georgia is a good place to do business, but also that production in Georgia will be more competitive than producing elsewhere and then exporting the product to Georgia or to other countries.

(5)   OUTLOOK

46.   The economy was badly shaken in 2008 as damage to infrastructure and disruption to activity in several sectors, including construction, trade, and tourism, severely dampened growth following the armed conflict with Russia. The on-going global economic crisis continues to threaten Georgia's growth prospects with lower commodity prices (in particular for fertilizers and metals), a drop in demand for Georgian exports, and a significant decline in private capital inflows, which have been the main driver of growth, all negatively affecting the economy. The Georgian authorities forecast a contraction in real GDP for 2009 of around 4% taking into account the declines in private capital inflows, exports, and remittances.

47.   According to the authorities, the current account deficit is likely to narrow in 2009 to around 16% of GDP (from the record high level of almost 23% in 2008). Exports and imports of goods and services are projected to decline by 20% and 27% respectively, reflecting flat import volumes and lower world oil prices, which will bring down the oil import bill; in addition, exchange rate depreciation is likely to discourage growth in consumer imports. On the other hand, the slowdown in trading partners is seen as keeping exports subdued in 2009, neutralizing the potential boost from a lower exchange rate. In particular, lower world demand for key commodity exports, such as copper and other metals, will dampen export earnings. FDI inflows, hitherto the main source of financing for the current account deficit and a principal driver of economic growth, are projected to be in the region of US$900 million for 2009, 40% lower than in 2008, depriving the economy of a significant source of growth. Flows of workers' remittances have also decreased as Russia (where the majority of Georgian working abroad are based) experiences a recession.

48.   Provided that a measure of regional stability can be re-established, the Georgian economy should experience higher growth rates from 2010 based on an expected recovery in exports and a significant recovery in FDI. Based on a moderate recovery of activity, the IMF forecasts real GDP growth at 2% in 2010 with the level of potential growth in the medium term remaining uncertain.[22] Inflation is expected to remain moderate at 3-5% in the medium term, down significantly from 11% at the end of 2007. The large amount of external aid granted to Georgia after the armed conflict could stimulate higher rates of consumption and investment, bringing about higher GDP growth. However, there are downside risks. Should a protracted period of political uncertainty (extending to the conduct of economic policy) ensue, foreign investors may shun Georgia for a longer period.

---

[22] IMF (2009c), p. 11.

49.   Structural reforms will be key both to further strengthening Georgia's resilience to shocks and to sustaining growth. When there is a recovery in external demand, structural reforms should help in attracting investment into export activities, improving productivity, thereby helping to create an enabling environment for export diversification.

II.   TRADE POLICY REGIME: FRAMEWORK AND OBJECTIVES

(1)   INTRODUCTION

1.   The November 2003 "Rose Revolution" and the ensuing election in 2004 brought to power a new Georgian administration, which has promoted a programme of political and economic reforms. Important among these were trade reforms, which included modernizing and reducing the size of the customs control institutions, simplifying the administrative requirements of customs clearance, unilaterally lowering import duties, and extending Georgia's involvement in international trade agreements. Substantial reforms have also been achieved in several other key areas, such as in improving the business and investment climate, increasing tax revenues, reforming government and public finance management, and fighting corruption. In 2007, domestic tensions led to demonstrations to which the Government responded with a brief period of martial law before early presidential elections were called in January 2008.

2.   Prior to the armed conflict of August 2008, the Georgian economy had displayed robust growth, partly due to the success of the reform process but the conflict led to a fall in investment and a serious decline in economic growth with increasing unemployment. It resulted in direct physical damage to the infrastructure – including to transport links, agriculture, tourism, and the environment – which was tangible but not large. Although the armed conflict lasted less than week, tensions remained, with Russia having occupied Abkhazia and South Ossetia – constituting approximately 20% of Georgian territory – and declaring their *de facto* separation from Georgia.

3.   In December 2008, the EU announced plans to enhance its relationship with Georgia (as well as Armenia, Azerbaijan, Moldova, and Ukraine) as part of a new Eastern Partnership that would involve gradual integration into the EU economy for countries that are willing and able to enter into a deeper engagement. The new partnership builds on the European Neighbourhood Policy framework, which has heavily influenced Georgian foreign trade policy since 2006, and envisages progressive regulatory approximation of Georgia's legislation and practises to the most important EU trade-related regulatory policy *acquis,* as well as the negotiation of a deep and comprehensive free-trade agreement.

(2)   INSTITUTIONAL FRAMEWORK

(i)   Branches of government

4.   An independent republic between 1918 and 1921, Georgia was incorporated into the Soviet Union in 1922, from which it declared its independence in April 1991. A new constitution, separating government into executive, legislative, and judicial branches, was approved in August 1995 and defined Georgia as a presidential republic.

5.   The President is the Head of State, elected by popular vote for a five-year term and may not hold office for more than two consecutive terms. The Constitution was amended in early 2004, resulting in the formation of a Cabinet and, for the first time, the creation of the post of Prime Minister. The PM, together with the ministers, is responsible for the day-to-day affairs of government. The PM's Office coordinates the position of Georgia in certain international economic negotiations including with the EU.

6.   The supreme legislative body is the unicameral *Sakartvelos Parlamenti* (Georgian Parliament), which is directly elected for four years. In March 2008, constitutional amendments reduced the number of deputies in the Parliament from 235 to 150, of whom 75 were to be elected on the basis of proportional representation and 75 in single-member constituencies. Parliament conducts

a vote of confidence on the presentation of the composition and programme of the Government and may impeach the President.

7.   Following the adoption of the Constitution, a new legal system was established with a Constitutional Court and a three-level system of common courts: (i) district (city) courts, which are the first instance courts under Article 15 of the Law of Georgia on Common Courts; (ii) appellate courts, where appeals on decisions of the first instance courts are submitted; and (iii) the Supreme Court of Georgia, which is the highest and final instance court for administering justice. Soviet laws have been replaced by new civil, administrative, and criminal codes. Since 2004, the Government has carried out a plethora of reforms concerning the judiciary and law-enforcement agencies. There has been substantial international support for court reform, and judges now have to pass tests before appointment. However, despite ongoing reforms aimed at encouraging transparency and impartiality in the judiciary, according to the Heritage Foundation and the U.S. Department of State it remains one of the least trusted institutions in Georgia and held in low esteem by the public.[1]

8.   Parliament is responsible for ratification of international treaties, while the President and the other executive authorities are responsible for implementation. Ratification was required to complete the national procedures relating to WTO accession. International treaties and agreements ratified by Parliament, including the WTO Agreement, have precedence over domestic laws and other acts in Georgia other than the Constitution and constitutional law. International agreements have direct applicability in the national legal system in accordance with Article 6 of the Constitution and Article 20 of the Law on Normative Acts. The hierarchy of normative acts in force comprises: (i) the Constitution of Georgia and the Constitutional Law of Georgia; (ii) international treaties and agreements ratified by Georgia; (iii) the Organic Law of Georgia; (iv) laws and presidential decrees; (v) orders of the President of Georgia; (vi) resolutions of the Parliament of Georgia; and (vii) orders of a minister or head of another central governmental authority of executive power. According to the authorities, Georgia's laws provide for the right to appeal administrative rulings on matters subject to WTO provisions to an independent tribunal, in conformity with WTO obligations.

(ii)   Regional issues

9.   In accordance with Article 3 of the Constitution, Georgia's supreme national bodies have exclusive authority to administer several trade-related areas, including customs and tariff regimes; foreign trade; standards and measurements, and sanitary measures at the border; legislation on banking, credit, insurance, and taxes; legislation on intellectual property; and legislation on trade, criminal law, civil law, and administrative and labour law. Sub-central entities within territory controlled by the Georgian Central Government have no autonomous authority over issues of subsidies, taxation, trade policy or any other measures covered by WTO provisions.

10.   Georgia applies WTO provisions uniformly throughout the entire customs territory controlled by the central Government, including in regions engaging in border trade or frontier traffic, special

---

[1] According to the U.S. Department of State, disputes over investors' rights have tended to undermine confidence in the impartiality of the Georgian judicial system and rule of law, and by extension, Georgia's investment climate. Both foreign and Georgian investors have expressed reservations about the competence, independence, and impartiality of court decisions. In some instances, for example, lower court decisions have changed control of property or of entire enterprises on questionable legal grounds and, in some cases, these decisions have been reversed by higher courts or government action. See U.S. Department of State (2008), p. 10. According to the Heritage Foundation, protection of property rights scores low, although the Georgian authorities point out that a new law on property legalization was adopted by Parliament in June 2007 with the aim of enhancing conditions for the irreversibility of granted/acquired property rights (Heritage Foundation, 2009).

economic zones, and other areas where special regimes for tariffs, taxes, and regulations are established. The autonomous regions of Abkhazia and South Ossetia are *de facto* not under the jurisdiction of the central Government and the local authorities do not apply the national customs tariff and other taxes.

11.   Following the August 2008 confrontation and in reaction to Russia's recognition of, and presence in, Abkhazia and South Ossetia, the Georgian Parliament passed a law, in December 2008, stipulating that the territories of the Autonomous Republic of Abkhazia and of the former Autonomous Republic of South Ossetia have the status of Occupied Territories. The law prohibits the following types of activities, or financing of such activities, in the territories: (a) any economic activity, regardless of whether it is implemented for profit, income or compensation, for which under the Georgian legislation a licence, permit, authorization, registration or agreement is required and has not been granted; (b) import and/or export of military products or products that have dual purpose; (c) international air traffic, maritime traffic, and railway traffic, also international automobile transportation of cargo; (d) use of natural resources; and (e) cash transfers. Without such permission, the authorities have confirmed that any goods presented to Customs will be stopped if they originate from, or are destined for, the occupied territories. According to press reports, Georgia has seized several foreign ships attempting to bring goods into Abkhazia and has detained a number of the ships' personnel.

(iii)   Institutional reforms: transparency, the anti-corruption agenda, and customs reform

12.   When it became independent from the Soviet Union, Georgia inherited a Soviet-style system of Government that was corrupt, over-staffed, and inefficient. Public disaffection with the situation resulted in the Rose Revolution, and the new Government promised to combat corruption, bring order to the Budget, and to reorient the economy towards privatization, free markets, and reduced regulation. In 2004, the Government started by radically reducing the size of executive Government. The number of ministries was reduced from 28 to 13, many state departments were abolished, and a large number of staff were either fired or required to re-apply for their old jobs in smaller departments. According to UNDP, the total number of public officials (120,000 in 2003) was cut in half by 2005.[2] In overhauling the administrative structure, the Government focused on those departments and ministries considered most corrupt, which included the police, judiciary, tax, and Customs. The remarkable success of government efforts in turning a nearly failed State into a maturing democracy can be seen in Georgia's rise up Transparency International's world rankings: in 2003, Georgia ranked 124th out of 133 countries surveyed on corruption; by 2008 it had moved up to 67th out of 180 countries.[3] According to the World Bank's "Anti-Corruption in Transition 3" report[4], Georgia topped the list of transitional countries in terms of anti-corruption efforts. The report reviewed the 2002-05 period and concluded that Georgia had achieved the largest reduction in corruption among all transition countries.

13.   The Heritage Foundation Economic Freedom Index ranks Georgia highly in terms of business, trade, and fiscal freedom but much lower for the legal system and the independence of the judiciary (Table AII.1). The European Parliament has noted that the privatization process has had

---

[2] UNDP (2008), p. 12.

[3] Transparency International Georgia (2003) and (2008b). In Transparency International's 2009 Global Corruption Barometer, which explores the public's view of corruption, 57% of the Georgians surveyed assessed the Government's actions in the fight against corruption as "effective", which is considerably higher than the average for newly independent states (21%) or even the EU (24%). The sector/organization considered to be the most affected by corruption was, by far, the judiciary (with 37%), followed by civil servants (21%), Parliament (16%), political parties (12%), and then business and the media.

[4] Cited in U.S. Department of State (2008), p. 13.

shortcomings in terms of transparency and irregularities and that the inflow of large amounts of donor funding may create additional incentives for corrupt behaviour.[5] Smuggling remains a serious obstacle to a competitive business environment and occurs largely as a result of the porous borders of the nation's separatist regions.[6] Georgia is not a signatory to the OECD Convention on Combating Bribery of Foreign Public Officials in International Business Transactions, but it acceded to the UN Anti Corruption Convention in November 2008.

14. Anti-corruption efforts have resulted in the arrest of former officials, the radical downsizing of state bureaucracies, crackdowns on smuggling, and have contributed to an increase in state revenue collections. The notoriously corrupt traffic police were completely disbanded in mid 2004. Georgian legislation provides for civil forfeiture of undocumented assets from public officials charged with corruption offences. Bribery is a criminal act under Georgian law, and Parliament recently accepted a package of constitutional amendments that make abuse of public office a criminal offence with a maximum penalty of 15-years imprisonment and confiscation of property.

15. The Georgian Government has made a commitment to greater transparency and simplicity of regulation. Laws and regulations are published in Georgian in the *Legislative Messenger,* the official gazette. The national anti-corruption strategy adopted in June 2004 was reinforced with an action plan in 2005 and an implementation plan in 2006; currently the Inter-Agency Coordination Council for Fighting Against Corruption is headed by the Minister of Justice. The legal framework has been strengthened with a new law on public procurement and the law on conflict of interest and corruption. Accountability mechanisms, such as the Chamber of Control and the Ombudsman, also help promote transparency and integrity in public service.

16. In the area of customs, unofficial administrative restrictions on trade have had negative effects: such as the time taken to process paperwork. High official or unofficial tariffs discouraged imports and therefore reduced competition, and higher import prices had a negative impact on import-dependent sectors. To counter such problems, the old Customs organization was dissolved after independence, and 80% of staff was recruited on the basis of short-term contracts. In April 2007, the institutions of tax and customs were further reorganized when the tax department, customs department and financial police were combined into a new State Revenue Service under the Ministry of Finance. The reform was targeted at reducing corruption, making the new organization more administratively efficient, and facilitating information sharing.

(3)   TRADE POLICY AND IMPLEMENTATION

(i)   Trade laws: key developments

17. Within the economic and structural reforms implemented by the Government, some of the most noteworthy measures have been in the trade area: tariff reform, combating corruption in customs; reform of the business licensing sector; regulatory reform of the financial sector; and the continuing adoption of trade-related legislation compatible with European and international standards,

---

[5] The EP notes that while the share of assistance that has gone into the pockets of corrupt officials or NGO activists is difficult to estimate, it is clear that every effort should be made to ensure appropriate use of EU funds (European Parliament, 2008).

[6] Georgia reasserted central control over the Black Sea region of Adjara in May 2004, reducing illicit economic activity there. However, the Georgian Government has raised concerns with Russia and with the international community about continued high levels of smuggling, money laundering, and even counterfeiting of U.S. dollars in the areas outside its control. The authorities state that Georgia's only request towards the Russian Federation in its WTO accession process has been the legalization and proper functioning of the two illegal customs check-points located on the Georgian-Russian border.

including in the area of standards and technical regulations, food safety, and competition. A number of obligations, mainly under the EU-Georgia Partnership and Cooperation Agreement (PCA) and European Neighbourhood Policy, have made a significant practical contribution towards Georgia's closer integration into the global economy.[7]

18.   The new customs code, effective January 2007, was designed to harmonize Georgia's customs legislation with EU legislation to make Georgian customs administration consistent with European rules.[8] The code aims to: encourage economic growth by increasing the volume of foreign trade, transit and processing on the basis of harmonized and simplified customs legislation; and support legal businesses through simplified customs procedures and by strengthening administrative measures against smuggling.

19.   At the start of the review period, more than 900 activities required a specific licence. This resulted in a large number of unlicensed businesses and, inevitably, corruption. In June 2005, Parliament passed a new law on licensing and Permits that cut 84% of existing licences and permits and reduced the number of cases where a licence is required to start or operate a business.

20.   European standards are considered the most relevant for Georgian economic development. Consequently, considerable work has taken place, some of it in the GEPLAC forum[9], in revising and harmonizing legislation as well as designing and implementing sound reform policies in several areas: agriculture and SPS measures; company law; competition; consumer protection; customs; financial services; intellectual property rights; public procurement; taxation; technical rules and standards; energy security; foreign direct investment; transport; and statistics.

(ii)   Main institutions

21.   Trade policy formulation and evaluation are under the overall responsibility of a governmental commission headed by the Prime Minister. The PM's office is also in charge of the negotiations and matters relating to the WTO and the EU-Georgia FTA process. Foreign trade and related issues fall largely under the purview of the Ministry of Economic Development (MoED). Other line ministries and agencies, such as the Ministry of Agriculture, the Ministry of Finance (including Customs) also play an important role in trade policy formulation and implementation.

22.   The main functions of the Department for Foreign Trade and International Economic Relations, within the MoED, include: participating in elaboration of the foreign-economic policy; cooperation with international organizations and regional entities; cooperation with donors in the framework of economic development and poverty reduction programmes; elaborating proposals for development of bilateral and multilateral trade relations; analysing implementation of obligations undertaken in international agreements and conventions, and preparing appropriate conclusions and proposals; analysing implementation of WTO commitments, and preparating proposals for trade

---

[7] The PCA, concluded in 1996, entered into force in 1999 and forms the legal basis of EU-Georgia relations. Respect for democracy, principles of international law, human rights, and market economy principles are the essential elements on which the EU-Georgia partnership is based.

[8] It is consistent with the customs code of the EU under the provisions of European Council Decree No. 2913/92, and with the EU customs code implementation provisions (Decree No. 2454/93).

[9] The Georgian European Policy and Legal Advice Centre (GEPLAC), funded by the European Union, renders high-level policy and legal advice to the Government and the Parliament of Georgia on a broad range of issues related to economic, legal, and institutional reform in the context of the implementation of the PCA between Georgia and the European Communities and their Member States. GEPLAC online information. Viewed at: http://www.geplac.org/eng.

legislation in order to be in line with WTO requirements; cooperation with European entities and elaborating proposals on Georgia's economic policy in line with EU requirements.

23.   The transport sector is under the responsibility of the Ministry of Economic Development and the Ministry of Regional Development and Infrastructure. The various transport activities are overseen by sectoral regulatory authorities. The Department for Information and Communication Technology within the MoED is responsible for policy in the telecommunications sector and for industrial policy in the field of electronic communications.

24.   Other relevant entities in, or attached to, the MoED include: the Department of Statistics[10]; the Department of Tourism and Resorts; and the Agency for Free Trade and Competition, the Georgia National Investment Agency (GNIA)[11], which provides a broad range of information and advice on the country to encourage foreign investors. The GNIA was established in 2002, under the National Investment Agency law, to act as a "one-stop-facility" for information about investment opportunities in Georgia. The Agency is the representative of the State to investors and will help in the negotiations with local government authorities to obtain appropriate licences and permission.

25.   The MoED also oversees the Restructuring Centre of Privatized Enterprises (CERMA), as well as the National Centre for Accreditation and the Georgian National Agency for Standards, Technical Regulations and Metrology. However, as of 2008, the Georgian State Procurement Agency is no longer under the auspices of the Ministry of Economy but is now accountable to the Prime Minister; this change was intended to better coordinate the work of the agency and avoid possible conflicts of interest as the MoED is itself a large procuring entity.

26.   Customs in Georgia is administered by the Customs Department of the State Revenue Service in the Ministry of Finance, it was set up in April 2007, by merging the tax administration with the customs administration and financial police, in order to improve coordination of these agencies.[12]

27.   The lead agency implementing IPR policy is the Georgian National Intellectual Property Centre (Sakpatenti), which deals with industrial property rights, patents, and appellations of origin; copyrights; and plant variety protection. Enforcement is carried out by the Ministry of the Interior, the financial police under the Ministry of Finance, and the Customs Department for trade-related matters.

28.   The Central Bank, the National Bank of Georgia (NBG), sets monetary policy. Until 2008, it issued licences and supervised the activities of banking institutions; these are now carried out by the Financial Supervision Agency, which supervises both banks and non-bank financial institutions.

29.   The Law on Facilitation and Guarantees of Investment Activities, passed in 1996, provides for equal treatment of Georgian and foreign investors and protects foreign investors from subsequent

---

[10] The relevant reform package to make it an independent agency is currently under discussion in Parliament.

[11] Georgian National Investment Agency. Viewed at: http://www.investingeorgia.org/doing_business/legislation.

[12] The Revenue Service is developing risk-based customs control and tax audit systems. In 2009, it will complete the implementation of the risk-management system and will initiate risk-assessment-based tax audits. For the full implementation of risk-based custom controls, a post-clearance system needs to be introduced. In this regard, amendments to the Customs Code were passed in December 2008 and new regulations on customs clearance have been in force since 1 January 2009. According to the authorities, staff were trained with the assistance of the USAID-financed Business Climate Reform project.

legislation that alters the condition of their investments for ten years.[13] Agricultural land can be purchased by forming a Georgian company that may be 100% foreign-owned.

(iii) Trade policy objectives

30. Basic Data and Directions (BDD) is the Government's key planning document and is updated annually under the coordination of the Ministry of Finance.[14] It contains overall government strategy and sectoral ministries' mission statements and priorities. The priority trade directions for 2008-11 are: (a) creating preferential foreign trade regimes with partner countries to diversify foreign trade markets; (b) developing technical regulations to make them consistent with international norms and thereby facilitate access to foreign markets and increase the competitiveness of goods and services produced in Georgia; and (c) increasing the attractiveness of Georgia for both foreign investment and tourism. According to the BDD, evaluation criteria include: rate of growth of foreign direct investments; diversification of foreign investment sources; rate of increase in the number of foreign tourists; and development of export diversification.

31. The authorities consider that further regulatory streamlining on several trade-related issues will help Georgia increase and diversify its exports. In this respect, the EU provides assistance on regulatory issues, notably technical regulations, standards and conformity assessment, sanitary and phytosanitary requirements, customs legislation and procedures, taxation, intellectual and industrial property rights, public procurements, etc. In many areas, Georgian legislation is already close to that of the EU. The most important challenges now are in the implementation of the adopted legislation. According to the EU, Georgia still lags behind in implementing its obligations under the ENP Action Plan, especially on competition policy, IPRs, product standards, and food safety. Regulatory convergence with European norms in these areas is of considerable importance for the reduction of non-tariff barriers in Georgia and for improving export capacity. The Georgian Banking Strategy for 2006-09 envisages harmonization of the Georgian banking framework with EU banking legislation, in accordance with the provisions of the EU/Georgia Action Plan.

(4) MAIN TRADE AGREEMENTS AND ARRANGEMENTS

(i) World Trade Organization

32. In June 1996, the Government of Georgia applied to join the World Trade Organization under Article XII of the Marrakech Agreement Establishing the WTO.[15] Georgia acceded in June 2000, the fourth former Soviet Republic to become a Member of the WTO (after the Kyrgyz Republic, Latvia, and Estonia). Georgia has most-favoured-nation trading relationships with all WTO member countries and benefits from the GSP schemes of the United States, Japan, Canada, Norway, and Switzerland and enjoys a GSP+ status with the European Union.

---

[13] Related legislation that has a bearing on foreign investment includes the Constitution, the Civil Code, the Tax Code, and the Customs Code, the Law on Entrepreneurs, the Bankruptcy Law, the Law on Courts and General Jurisdiction, the Law on Limitation of Monopolistic Activity, the Accounting Law, and the Securities Market Law. The legal framework governing ownership and privatization of property is established by: the Civil Code, the Law on Ownership of Agricultural Land, the Law on Private Ownership of Non-Agricultural Land, the Law on Management of State-Owned Non-Agricultural Land, and the Law on Privatization of State Property. Property rights in the extractive industries are governed by the Law on Concessions, the Law on Deposits and the Law on Oil and Gas. Financial-sector legislation includes the Law on Commercial Banks, the Law on National Banks, and the Law on Insurance Activities.

[14] For the latest document see Government of Georgia (2007), especially pp. 55-56.

[15] See the notification in WTO online information. Viewed at: http://www.wto.org/english/thewto_e/countries_e/georgia_e.htm.

33.   In addition to the mandatory WTO agreements, Georgia joined a number of sectoral initiatives, which stipulated zero import tariffs in: civil aircraft and information technology, pharmaceutical products, metal products, wood products and agricultural machinery. Georgia also agreed to start negotiations on joining the Government Procurement Agreement. To accelerate the accession process, Georgia agreed to have no transitional period for the TRIPS Agreement or the GATS. Under the GATS, Georgia applied its domestic regulations to, and did not discriminate against, foreign suppliers in, *inter alia,* banking, insurance, securities trade, auditing, legal services, and tourism. Also, Georgia negotiated the Aggregate Measure of Support for agriculture at 5% of agricultural GDP, corresponding to the obligations of a developed country.

34.   Georgia's main interest in the DDA negotiations is a fair, inclusive, and predictable trading environment where trade-distorting measures, especially in the agriculture sector are eliminated. At the same time, Georgia attaches importance to non-agriculture market access; it has not made an initial offer in the services negotiations, considering that it undertook extensive unilateral liberalization at the time of its accession. Protection of the rights of Georgian wine producers is a priority and in this respect Georgia actively supports proposals in the DDA framework to establish a multilateral register of geographical indications, of which Georgia is co-sponsor.[16]

35.   As a Member, Georgia is required to make periodic notifications under the various WTO Agreements (Table AII.2). Notifications are processed mainly in the Ministry of Foreign Affairs.

(ii)   Commonwealth of Independent States (CIS)

36.   Georgia has a free-trade regime with members of Commonwealth of Independent States (CIS) whose other members are: Azerbaijan, Armenia, Belarus, Kazakhstan, Kyrgyzstan, Moldova, Russia, Tajikistan, Turkmenistan, Uzbekistan, and Ukraine. The CIS countries have traditionally been Georgia's largest trade partners and although their share of trade with Georgia has declined, they still accounted for 36% of exports and 33% of imports in 2008. In August 2009, Georgia terminated its membership of the CIS organization[17] while maintaining its right to remain a member of the CIS free-trade-area arrangements and the bilateral agreements.

37.   In 1994, Georgia signed an FTA with other CIS member states that envisaged the trading of goods without customs tariffs. It was ratified by all the CIS member countries except Russia.[18] However, the FTA remained ineffectual and, as a result, preferential trading relations among CIS countries have been established and determined in bilateral free-trade agreements. Georgia has bilateral FTAs with Russia, Azerbaijan, Turkmenistan, Armenia, Ukraine, and Kazakhstan (all ratified and notified to the WTO), and Moldova and Uzbekistan (neither ratified nor notified). The Georgia-Russia FTA has been suspended since October 2006 when Russia closed its land frontier and civil aviation connections with Georgia and banned the import of wines and agriculture products.

38.   The bilateral agreements are more or less identical and provide for duty-free trade in goods (both industrial and agricultural); exemptions are contained in the protocols to the FTAs and can be changed annually. The FTAs do not cover trade in services, investment or government procurement. They contain provisions on contingent protection measures, including quotas, export taxes, safeguards, and anti-dumping measures, which countries can apply unilaterally.

---

[16] WTO documents TN/C/W/52 and Add.2.

[17] Georgia terminated its membership of the 1991 Agreement on the formation of the CIS, the 1993 CIS Charter, and the 1993 Agreement on the creation of economic relations.

[18] Georgia notified the WTO on 2 April 2003.

(iii)   European Union (EU)

39.   Relations between the EU and Georgia started in 1992, when Georgia regained its sovereignty after the break-up of the Soviet Union, and bilateral relations have further intensified since 2004. The legal foundation for EU-Georgia relations is the Partnership and Cooperation Agreement (PCA), negotiated at the same time as Georgia's WTO accession, and entering into force in 1999. According to Article 1 of the PCA, the agreement is aimed at fostering cooperation, on trade, political, environmental, and cultural issues. The PCA regulates political dialogue, trade, investment, economic, legislative, and cultural cooperation. It envisages progressive regulatory approximation of Georgia's legislation and practises to the most important EU trade-related regulatory *acquis*. This is aimed at ensuring better access for Georgian products to the EU market. Through the PCA, which also eliminates trade quotas and strengthens the protection of intellectual, industrial and commercial property rights, the parties have accorded each other MFN treatment, and Georgia benefits from the EU's General System of Preferences (GSP).

40.   In 2005, the EU provided Georgia with an expanded opportunity to make use of tariff privileges (under GSP plus), enabling Georgia to export about 7,200 items to the EU market with zero tariff rates. Previously Georgia was allowed to export only 3,300 products without any customs duty and 3,900 products under certain preferences. Georgia qualifies for the enhanced preferences for good governance and sustainable development and, in order to continue benefiting from the system after January 2009, Georgia ratified the two outstanding conventions listed in GSP regulations, namely the UN Convention on Anti-Corruption, and the Cartagena Protocol on Biosafety. As a result Georgia was granted the Special Incentive Arrangements under GSP Plus for 2009-11.

41.   In June 2004, Georgia joined the European Neighbourhood Policy (ENP) and in October 2006 an ENP Action Plan for Georgia was agreed for a period of five years.[19] The implementation of the ENP has been guided and monitored on the basis of annual implementation tools, which set out comprehensive priorities and time lines agreed jointly by the EU and Georgia. According to the Office of the State Minister of Georgia for European and Euro-Atlantic Integration, "today Georgia's foreign policy more than ever is directed towards the EU, which is largely perceived as guarantor of peace, democracy, development, stability, territorial integrity and human rights protection".[20] In July 2004, the Georgian Government adopted a decree establishing a Commission for Georgia's integration into the EU, chaired by the Prime Minister. The Commission's aims are, *inter alia*, to facilitate PCA implementation and participation in the ENP.

42.   In July 2007, the European Commission and Georgia started the negotiation process for an agreement on protection of geographical indications of agricultural products and foodstuff, and in April 2008, reached agreement on mutual recognition and protection of agricultural products and other foodstuffs. According to the authorities, the agreement is expected to be finalized in the fourth quarter of 2009.

43.   In December 2008, the European Commission announced plans to enhance its relationship with Georgia (as well as Armenia, Azerbaijan, Moldova, and Ukraine) as part of a new Eastern Partnership that would involve the gradual integration into the EU economy for Eastern Partnership countries that were willing and able to enter into a deeper engagement.

44.   Based on the progress made in the ENP, the Eastern Partnership – consisting of EU27 and Armenia, Azerbaijan, Belarus, Georgia, Republic of Moldova, and Ukraine – offers both bilateral and

---

[19] EC Commission (2006).

[20] Office of the State Minister of Georgia for European and Euro-Atlantic Integration (2009), p. 2.

multilateral measures for enhanced cooperation. According to the Commission[21], Georgia, as well the other partner countries, can align themselves more closely to the EU, depending on their individual capabilities and time frames with the signing of Association Agreements also planned in this framework. Regarding trade and regulatory approximation, the Commission is proposing, *inter alia:* assistance concerning administrative capacity development in areas such as SPS rules, customs and trade facilitation, taxation, intellectual and industrial property rights, public procurement, competition, and services, including financial services; support for the creation of a network of bilateral deep and comprehensive free-trade areas with partner countries; cooperation on enforcement of IP protection, in particular as regards counterfeited and pirated goods; exploration of possibilities for partners to participate in a system of diagonal cumulation of origin; and increased cooperation on customs and trade facilitation and border management to ensure a smooth flow of goods and enhance security and safety, and to combat customs fraud.

45.   On the possibility of setting up a deep and comprehensive free-trade agreement between the EU and Georgia, the European Commission tendered an independent feasibility study in 2007, which concluded that Georgia would benefit from such an agreement and needed to make further efforts in trade-related areas to prepare for the far-reaching liberalization involved.[22]   Following the extraordinary European Council of 1 September 2008, which concluded that "the EU should step up relations with Georgia, including the possible establishment of a full and comprehensive free-trade area as soon as the conditions are met" a preparatory process has been launched to help Georgia achieve the necessary level of preparedness for the DCFTA negotiating process.[23]

(iv)   Turkey

46.   GSP plus privileges granted by Turkey were replaced by a free-trade agreement between Georgia and the Republic of Turkey, which was signed on 21 November 2007 and entered into force on 1 November 2008. The Agreement was notified to the WTO under Article XXIV of the GATT 1994 on 18 February 2009.[24] According to this agreement, customs tariffs on industrial products have been fully eliminated but a number of agricultural products are excluded by both parties and some are subject to tariff quotas by Turkey. Furthermore, it does not cover services and investment, and does not go beyond WTO requirements on regulatory issues. The FTA is set to facilitate the development of trade and economic relations between the two countries, encourage entrepreneurs to gain access to new markets, and support implementation of investment projects.

(v)   United States

47.   In June 2007, Georgia and the United States signed a Trade and Investment Framework Agreement (TIFA) to address trade issues and build trade and investment relations. The TIFA sets up a joint U.S.-Georgia Council on Trade and Investment that will address a wide range of trade and investment issues including trade capacity building, intellectual property, labour, and environment. The Council will also help to increase commercial and investment opportunities by identifying and working to remove impediments to trade and investment flows between the United States and Georgia. A GSP statute was granted by the United States to Georgia, and in January 2009 Georgia signed the Georgia-US Charter on Strategic Partnership which, *inter alia,* will update the bilateral

---

[21] EC Commission (2008).

[22] CASE (2008).

[23] EC Commission (2009). In this regard, the Georgian authorities have stated that European Commission fact-finding mission visited Georgia in October 2008 to discuss trade issues. Based on the mission's recommendations, the Georgian Government has created an FTA task force, headed by the PM's office, to take specific actions to be prepared for the start of DCFTA negotiations.

[24] WTO document WT/REG26/N/1, 24 February 2009.

investment treaty, expand Georgian access to the GSP, and explore the possibility of a free-trade agreement.

(vi)   Other agreements

48.   A key economic policy objective for Georgia is to capitalize on its strategic geographic location between the Caspian and the Black Sea, linking Asia and Europe. Major oil and gas pipelines, such as the BTC and South Caucasus pipeline, roads, railways, and communications along the East-West corridor transit Georgian territory and are considered important assets for its future prosperity. To this end, Georgia is a member of the Black Sea Economic Cooperation Pact and a four-country grouping of Georgia, Ukraine, Azerbaijan, and Moldova (GUAM).[25] GUAM is important for Georgia as it plays a role in strengthening regional cooperation, a role that has been enhanced since Georgia applied to leave the CIS.

49.   Georgia has two key regional cooperation priorities: transport and trade facilitation; and energy trade. Firstly, Georgia has prioritized its participation in the Eurasian transport corridor project supported by the European Union. The project links Central Asia and Europe through the Caucasus. Development of these corridors will enable Georgia to realize its full transit economy potential. The Government's objective is to combine high-quality transport infrastructure (roads, railways, ports) with trade facilitation, including harmonization of border crossing procedures, transit fees, and tariffs. Secondly, Georgia, Azerbaijan, and Turkey cooperate on energy security and energy transportation. In this context, Georgia has significant hydro-energy potential and export opportunities and is seeking private investment in this sector.

(5)   TRADE DISPUTES AND CONSULTATIONS

50.   Georgia has not been involved in any direct or indirect trade disputes in the WTO between 1995 and March 2009. However, Georgia's trade relations with Russia have been problematic since 2004, severely limiting trade and transport between the two. In 2005 and 2006, Russia banned imports of Georgian agricultural products, mineral water, and wine, for which Russia was Georgia's largest market. In September 2006, Russia cut all direct transport links with Georgia. Gazprom, the Russian gas monopoly, doubled the price of natural gas supplied to Georgia but new supplies of natural gas from Azerbaijan and increased hydroelectric generating capacity are making Georgia much less dependent on Russian energy sources.

(6)   FOREIGN INVESTMENT REGIME

51.   Georgia's investment legislation aims to open the Georgian economy to increased international business activity, and to help create a business environment favourable to foreign investment. The 1996 Law on Investment Activity Promotion and Guarantees ensures that foreign investors may invest on a national-treatment basis in any sector open to private investment with up to

---

[25] The Black Sea Economic Cooperation (BSEC) agreement became operational in 1999. It comprises Georgia and ten other members: Albania, Armenia, Azerbaijan, Bulgaria, Greece, Moldova, Romania, Russia, Turkey, and Ukraine. Although the BSEC provides for cooperation in various fields, it does not provide for preferential tariff concessions. The areas of cooperation include banking and finance, and exchange of statistical data and economic information regarding energy, transport, telecommunication, trade and industry, agriculture and agri-industry, environmental protection, tourism, and science and technology. GUAM is designed to foster favourable trade conditions among member states and strengthen economic links between them. In May 2006, Ukraine and Azerbaijan announced plans to further develop GUAM member relations by renaming the organization GUAM Organisation for Democracy and Economic Development and establishing its headquarters in the Ukrainian capital.

100% foreign ownership; the few strategically significant exceptions include defence and security.[26] Georgian law guarantees the right of an investor to convert and repatriate capital and profits after payment of all required taxes, and provides a ten-year guarantee against adverse legislative changes and the possibility to apply international practice in dispute resolution.[27] In addition, the Law on State Promotion of Investments covers investments of over GEL 8 million, or those having significant influence on economic or infrastructure development.[28]

52.   Investors' rights are detailed in Georgia's bilateral investment agreements. According to the authorities, Georgia has negotiated bilateral agreements on investment promotion and mutual protection with Armenia, Austria, Azerbaijan, Belgium, Bulgaria, China, Egypt, France, Germany, Greece, Iran, Israel, Italy, Kazakhstan, Kyrgyzstan, Latvia, Lithuania, Moldova, Netherlands, Romania, Turkey, Turkmenistan, Ukraine, United Kingdom, United States, and Uzbekistan. Internal procedures have been completed and drafts are being negotiated with the Governments of Bangladesh, Bosnia, Croatia, Cyprus, Czech Republic, Denmark, Herzegovina, Iceland, India, Indonesia, Kuwait, Lebanon, Malta, Norway, Philippines, Saudi Arabia, Slovak Republic, Slovenia, Switzerland, and Tajikistan.

53.   According to the Ministry of Finance as of July 2009, Georgia has 26 double taxation treaties in force (with 17 EC countries and with Armenia, Azerbaijan, China, Iran, Japan, Kazakhstan, Turkmenistan, Ukraine, and Uzbekistan). Four treaties await ratification (with Russia, Turkey, Luxemburg, and Ireland), and nine are being negotiated (with Switzerland, Malta, Spain, Kuwait, Cyprus, Singapore, Israel, Slovenia, and Hungary).

(7)   TECHNICAL ASSISTANCE

(i)   Assistance provided

54.   According to the joint WTO/OECD database, from 2001 to 2007, Georgia benefited from trade-related assistance funded by international institutions and bilateral donors, to the tune of US$119.1 million.[29] Assistance was significantly increased in 2006 when Georgia received almost US$47 million, mainly in the form of grants and concessional loans, with a major contribution from the United States through its business climate reform project. Beyond WTO-related trade issues, Georgia receives assistance from, *inter alia,* the United States, the European Union and international institutions to promote democratic reform, resolve regional conflicts, foster energy independence, assist economic development, and reduce poverty. In addition, Georgia attaches great importance to targeted assistance to help strengthen human resource capacities in the private sector and diversify its economy, focusing on high-value products, optimization of energy resources, and development of telecommunications, transport, and infrastructure.

---

[26] Investment prohibitions concern: creation, production, and proliferation of WMDs and construction of their test ranges; import of nuclear and toxic waste materials; scientific work related to human cloning; and production of drugs. Investments permitted only for the State include production of money and postal stamps; and production of and trade in drugs for medical purposes.

[27] See Articles 15 (Guarantees during amendment of legislation) and 16 (Procedure for dispute resolution) of the Law of Georgia on Investment Activity Promotion and Guarantees. Viewed at: http://mfa.gov.ge/files70_9428_624394_60_69_132776_LawonInvestm.Prom.pdf.

[28] See Georgian National Investment Agency online information. Viewed at: http://www.investingeorgia.org/ doing_business/legislation/.

[29] Joint WTO/OECD TRTA/CB database, *Beneficiary Country: Georgia.* Viewed at: http://tcbdb.wto.org/benef_country.aspx.

55.   Since its accession to the WTO (to mid 2009) Georgia has participated in 132 trade-related technical assistance activities organized both by the WTO and partner institutions. At the regional level, Georgia has participated in over 70 activities organized either by the WTO or other partners like the Joint Vienna Institute, the Black Sea Economic Cooperation organization, the OECD, the World Bank, the Asian Development Bank, and the International Development Law Organisation. Subjects covered in these regional activities included: agriculture; trade negotiation skills, NAMA, services, trade facilitation, trade and environment, government procurement, TRIPS, RTAs, rules of origin, TBT, dispute settlement, and international trade law. In addition, Georgia benefited from the Netherlands Trainee Programme in 2005.

56.   Georgia has also benefited from a number of TA activities on TRIPS. Recent activities include participation in a regional seminar in 2006 related to the TRIPS Agreement and public health, designed to assist Georgia and the economies of the region in implementing and making effective use of the mechanism established under the WTO Decision on Paragraph 6 of the Doha Declaration on the TRIPS Agreement and Public Health, as recently transposed into the Protocol amending the TRIPS Agreement. In June 2008, a workshop for Central and Eastern European and Central Asian and the Caucasus (CEECAC) countries covered topics such as public health, biotechnology, biodiversity, traditional knowledge, and geographical indications. Furthermore, Georgia is currently cooperating with UNDP to study the circulation of pirated and counterfeit products in Georgia for which accurate data is lacking. Georgia has benefited from the EU-funded Technical Assistance and Information Exchange (TAIEX) project in terms of study visits and seminars on various IP subjects.

57.   Georgia participated in regional seminars on competition policy organized in the CEECAC region in 2000 and 2003. In 2006, Georgia benefited from a development grant of US$9.6 million from the Millennium Challenge Corporation, aimed at supporting and reinforcing competition institutions as well as providing assistance in preparing draft legislation on competition. Georgia has also benefited from TA activities related to public procurement and the GPA, and has participated in the WTO global seminars on GPA, most recently in 2008.[30] Georgia has expressed particular interest in ongoing training on supervision, monitoring, and administrative reviews of public procurement, including e-procurement procedures.

58.   In the context of assistance given to Georgia on trade facilitation, several organizations and donors provided support in the area of customs valuations and tariff reform, including the IMF, UNCTAD, the United States, and the EU. These projects cover essentially the modernization of the custom administration by improving efficiency through the upgrading of the customs infrastructure and the training of customs officers.

59.   Georgia has benefited from TA delivered by organizations and bilateral donors on standards-related issues. In 2002 and 2003, for example, UNDP provided a grant of US$400,000 to support Georgian exporters through improvement of quality control and certification systems, including the introduction of ISO standards to help Georgian exporters meet international quality requirements and environmental standards. In 2006, the USAID SME Support Project provided technical assistance and financial support to improve standards for the export goods.

60.   More generally, Georgia has benefited from a number of WTO training courses for government officials in the form of the short trade policy course for CEECAC countries; specialized

---

[30] The objectives of this global workshop organized at the WTO headquarters are: (i) to enhance participants' knowledge and awareness of the concepts, principles, and obligations as well as the coverage-related aspects of the Agreement on Government Procurement (including both the existing Agreement and the provisionally revised text of December 2006 (GPA/W/297)); and (ii) to facilitate policy development and decision-making at the national level.

courses on a number of WTO issues; and the regional trade negotiating course. Georgia wishes to continue to benefit from such training to enhance trade capacity within government ministries and agencies involved in trade policy formulation and the negotiation of trade agreements.

(ii)   Technical assistance needs

61.   Georgia is currently carrying out a comprehensive assessment of its technical assistance needs in the trade area, not only in the context of its WTO membership but also within the framework of its evolving trading relationship with the EU. New obligations for implementation arising out of the DDA may further challenge already stretched resources. Support from the international community could assist Georgia in achieving greater integration into the multilateral trading system.

62.   Georgia's concerns relate, *inter alia,* to implementation issues attributed to constraints in capacity, know-how, and skills in the various agencies involved. Two prominent areas are standards/SPS measures and intellectual property protection. Georgia could benefit from technical assistance to help develop its resources and further develop its standards institutions. As it moves further towards international practices for standards, technical regulations, and conformity assessment, the authorities indicated the need to increase the level of expertise to enhance their participation in regulatory and international standard-setting activities, including effective participation in the TBT Committee. Officials involved in the development of national standards, for instance, could benefit from improved training, monitoring and surveillance capacity, and performance in the area of notifications in both TBT and SPS matters. Assistance is needed to increase capacities to submit notifications on SPS measures more effectively and to establish better communication channels with relevant stakeholders. The authorities have also emphasized the importance of having a dedicated physical location (enquiry point) with appropriate equipment based at the Ministry of Agriculture to ensure proper handling of notifications.

63.   While Georgia has enacted a great deal of the legislation necessary to be fully compliant with the TRIPS Agreement, limited administrative capacity in a number of IPR-related areas is a significant obstacle to implementation. Additional training on TRIPS, in particular on issues pertaining to parallel imports for products other than pharmaceuticals, and how this is regulated by other WTO Members, and on enforcement issues, would be beneficial. Georgia needs to raise awareness among the different IP right-holders and improve training for enforcement officials (customs officers, judges, etc.).

64.   Other areas that would likely benefit from short-term targeted technical assistance and capacity-building programmes include (in no particular order of priority): need for additional support in training customs officers in identifying pirated and counterfeit goods at the border as well as specialized training in audit techniques and post clearance control; upgrading of the reference centre (RC), established in 2001 in the Ministry of Foreign Affairs, in order to use it for accessing official WTO information as well as to train officials via the WTO e-training course.

III. TRADE POLICIES AND PRACTICES BY MEASURE

(1) INTRODUCTION

1. Since independence, the overriding objective of Georgia's economic policies has been to create and develop a market economy through privatization of state-owned commercial enterprises, deregulation of prices, and liberalization of its trade and investment regimes. Much of this had been achieved by Georgia's accession to the WTO in 2000; Georgia had established the legislative basis for competitive markets by liberalizing prices, rescinding exclusive rights granted to certain economic agents, abolishing restrictions on competition in certain activities, and cutting subsidized credits to state-owned enterprises. Trade and trade-related policies pursued during the review period have built on these achievements, helping to harmonize Georgia's trade and related legislation with international norms, by introducing or amending legislation in areas such as customs administration and tariffs, import licensing, intellectual property protection, standardization and certification, government procurement, privatization, competition, and business legislation.

2. Georgia has streamlined its customs procedures and continued to liberalize its trade regime. Import tariffs were significantly reduced in 2006, making Georgia's applied MFN tariff rate – at 1.5% – one of the lowest worldwide, and the number of tariff bands was reduced from sixteen to three; nearly 86% of imported goods currently enter Georgia duty free. As a consequence, the contribution of tariffs in trade tax revenues declined from 32% to under 3% between 1998 and 2008, although excise taxes and VAT ensured that taxes collected on imports maintained a significant share (around one third) of total tax revenue. There is effectively no tariff escalation nor any evident tariff peaks, and Georgia has no quantitative restrictions on trade. The import licensing system was simplified in 2005 when the number of licences required for import and export was substantially reduced, with licensing required only to protect public health and the environment and ensure national security. Georgia does not apply contingency measures and has no relevant legislation for such measures. There are minimal export restrictions in terms of export taxes or licensing, no export subsidies nor any government financing for exporters other than bank loans at market interest rates.

3. Government procurement, which accounts for about one sixth of GDP, has been further liberalized with the phasing out of preferences for domestic bidders. Legislative amendments currently under consideration aim to increase transparency through the introduction of electronic procurement. Regarding standards and SPS requirements, Georgia has made major legislative and institutional changes in its transition from a centrally planned to a market economy but faces a number of implementation problems particularly in regard to food safety. Although Georgia has adopted a number of new basic laws over recent years covering food safety, veterinary, and plant protection issues, minimum international standards for food safety have not yet been achieved, and the sector lacks funding to ensure adequate nationwide food-safety structures.

4. The business environment has undergone a sea change in recent years with the number of business activities subject to licences and permits reduced by over 80% since 2005, a feature that has been important in attracting foreign investment. There are also special taxation regimes for international financial companies, international companies operating in free industrial zones, and free warehouse companies, which exempt them from profit and property tax. Significant privatization of formerly state-owned enterprises has been achieved in recent years, and the Government received over US$1.4 billion in revenue between 2005 and 2008, mainly in telecommunications, energy, large-scale real estate assets, and the health sector.

5. Competition law was overhauled in 2005 with the focus on the prohibition of state aid and subsidies although, in the view of some observers, the law does not apply sufficiently to agreements

restricting competition, concerted practices, abuse of dominant position, and state enterprises. Intellectual property legislation exists across several IP areas including patents, trade marks, copyright, and geographical indications, but continuing resource and capacity constraints appear to be the main hindrances to effective implementation.

(2) MEASURES DIRECTLY AFFECTING IMPORTS

(i) Customs documentation and administration

(a) Documentation

6. According to the Customs Code (Article 15, paragraph 2), the documents required for customs control and/or customs supervision are defined by Orders of the Minister of Finance. Under Order No. 1760 import documentation must include: the Cargo Customs Declaration, and the appropriate transport document (for motor transport: TIR Carnet, CMR, or vehicle registration document; for air transport: airway bill; for sea transport: bill of lading, consignment note, letter of conveyance; and for carriage via rail transport: railway bill of lading, waybill). The contract, or commercial invoice is also required, but if importer does not have this document, the declared goods are allowed into the country but are subject to 100% physical inspection. If the importer wishes to claim tax exemption based on the origin of the goods, a preferential certificate of origin needs to be presented. Importers of goods subject to non-tariff measures must present relevant documentation (such as permission, licence or certificate of conformity). According to Order No. 1770 the same procedure applies for export, although a contract or commercial invoice is not obligatory.

(b) Administration

7. After Independence, Georgian Customs had to overcome a number of serious problems: the need to build a post-Soviet system from scratch, the absence of *de facto* Georgian jurisdiction over South Ossetia and Abkhazia, poor management, and rampant bribery and corruption in the customs and tax administration. Customs reform was therefore an important priority on the reform agenda, and radical changes have been made to customs and tax legislation in recent years. A new tax code entered into force on 1 January 2005 and a new customs code on 1 January 2007 following a far-reaching review of tax and customs policies with a view to introducing a more liberal regime. Out of 21 taxes under the previous regime, only six still exist, of which three – customs tax, excise tax, and VAT directly affect imports.[1] Administration has also been helped by a simplified tariff.

Legislation

8. The Customs Code of Georgia (CCG) regulates customs procedures.[2] It defines various customs regimes under which goods are brought in or taken out of the customs territory of Georgia. The revision was aimed at simplifying customs procedures and harmonizing both customs legislation and procedures with the European Community Customs Code and the revised Kyoto Convention on the Simplification and Harmonisation of Customs Procedures. Significant changes between the revised code and the previous regime include[3]:

---

[1] Five (personal income tax, corporate income tax, VAT, excise tax, and customs duties) are state-wide, and one (property tax) is a local tax.
[2] Customs Code of Georgia (unofficial English translation by the American Chamber of Commerce). Viewed at: http://www.amcham.ge/res/Bullets_on_1stPage/CUSTOMS_CODE_OF_GEORGIA_ENG.doc.
[3] Georgian Law Review (2005).

- Explicit definition: customs procedures from the time of crossing the border up to the release of goods are unambiguously defined; also incorporation of customs implementing provisions (definitions relating to customs tariffs, classification of goods, determination of origin and customs valuation), previously scatted over different regulations, etc.

- Reduction in the number of customs procedures from 15 to 7. The revised list of customs procedures, based on international best practice, comprises: release of goods for free circulation (import); transit of goods; customs warehousing of goods; inward processing of goods; temporary admission of goods; outward processing of goods; and export.[4]

- Reduction in the number of documents needed for export and import registration.

- Provision for the importer to amend particulars of a customs declaration, in case of minor technical mistakes, without having to pay, as well as possibility to defer the payment of a customs debt for one month.

- Introduction of a bond/guarantee system, to allow officials to suspend the payment of duty and taxes pending the completion of an authorized activity.

- Provisions on free zones and free warehouses in contrast to the previous customs code; provision for customs appeals and penalties were brought into line with the tax code, including definition of customs violations.

9.   In 2008, a number of important amendments were made to the Code, dealing with issues such as valuation, nomenclature, post clearance audit, simplified customs procedures for authorized operators, binding tariff and origin information, and warehouses. The authorities state that further legislation required for the correct implementation of the Customs Code is under way.[5]

Procedures

10.   Procedures for importing goods have been significantly simplified and improvements are on-going. The European Commission's assessment of customs in Georgia noted that there had been positive developments since 2007 in the customs declaration system and on coordination of technical regulations as well as in the clarification of the customs code to tackle corruption in the areas of valuation, post-clearance audit, and warehouse approvals.[6] However, in the Commission's view, the lack of clear implementing provisions to the code has complicated the implementation of valuation rules as well as of post clearance controls. In response to this view, the authorities noted that new detailed secondary legislation has extensively revised customs valuation regulations and the implementation of post-clearance customs audit.

---

[4] The term "Customs-approved treatment or use" was also introduced in the CCG and refers to: the placement of goods under a customs procedure; entry of goods into a free zone or free warehouse; re-exportation of goods from the customs territory of Georgia; destruction of goods under customs supervision, and transfer of goods into the ownership of the State.

[5] On the basis of the latest amendments of the CCG, which entered into force in 2009, a number of additional acts need to be adopted: the Decree on the Georgia Integrated Tariff; the MoF Order on National Commodity Nomenclature of Foreign Economic Activity (in order to switch to HS2007); Mof Order on rules of implementation of post-clearance customs audit; the MoF Order on Advance Customs Ruling; and the Joint Order (MoF and Ministry of Interior) on Rules of Entrance, Movement and Leaving in Customs Control Zone of Border Crossing Points Open to International Movement.

[6] EC Commission (2009), p. 5.

11.   Tax and customs were consolidated into a single department in 2007: the Revenue Service of the Ministry of Finance of Georgia (RS). The RS has begun developing risk-based customs control and tax audit systems and, since March 2008, a risk-based checking system is operational at customs check-points. The risk assessment is performed on the basis of ASYCUDA and its supplementary software using the price discrepancy and importers/exporters risks analysis. The risk-based checking system significantly reduces the time taken for customs clearance procedures, as well as administrative resources.

12.   In 2009, according to the Georgian authorities, the RS will complete finish the implementation of the risk-management system and will initiate risk-assessment-based tax audits. To facilitate the full implementation of risk-based custom controls, a post-clearance system has been introduced in 2009.

(ii)   Tariffs and other charges affecting imports

(a)   Overview of trade taxes

13.   In 2008, taxes collected on imports accounted for nearly 38% of tax revenues compared with around 32% in 2004 and 1998 (Table III.1). The contribution of customs duties (tariffs) has decreased both in nominal and relative terms, in line with a decline in the effective import tariff rate, and by 2008 accounted for under 3% of total trade taxes, down from 32% ten years earlier. Excise taxes on imports have maintained a relatively constant share of around 22% whereas VAT on imports now accounts for the lion's share of taxes on imports.

Table III.1
Taxation of imports, 1998, 2001, 2004 and 2008

	1998	2001	2004	2008
Total taxes on imports as percent of total tax revenues	32.3	29.3	32.6	37.6
Composition of trade taxes (as percent of total)				
Custom duties	32.0	19.8	15.9	2.9
Excise tax on imports	20.1	24.5	26.0	22.7
VAT on imports	47.9	55.7	58.1	74.4
Share of taxes on imports in total collection of the given tax (%)				
Excise tax	92.7	76.2	69.6	76.4
VAT	44.9	43.6	58.1	76.4

Source: Figures for 1998 and 2001 cited in Word Bank (2003), *Georgia – An Integrated Trade Development Strategy,* Report No. 27264-GE, p. 20, November. Figures for 2004 and 2008 supplied by the Georgian authorities.

(b)   Tariffs

14.   Under 2006 amendments to the customs system, import tariffs were significantly reduced making Georgia's tariff rates among the lowest in the world. The low tariff reduces the need for exemptions and drawbacks to mitigate the adverse effect of tariffs on exports, insofar as tariffs are levied on intermediate inputs used to produce goods for export. In addition to combating corruption, the most obvious impact of the unilateral improvements in access to the Georgian market was to make business, and particularly importing, easier. According to the World Bank, Georgia has made exceptional progress in simplifying the documentation requirements for import and export and decreasing the cost of trade (Table I.3).[7]

15.   Until 2006, the tariff was characterized by relatively high rates (up to 30%) and numerous (16) bands, which was not competitive in the region and not supportive of an attractive business

---

[7] World Bank (2009a).

climate in the country. High tariffs, *inter alia,* increased prices on products of common consumption, and the 16 different rates made customs procedures difficult and open to corruption. As a result of a revised law on customs tariffs (Law of Georgia No. 3509, subsequently moved into the Tax Code), the tariff system was substantially changed in September 2006, and the number of tariff bands was reduced to three. The changes lowered tariff barriers substantially, with the simple average MFN tariff estimated at 1.5%, down from 7.2%.

16.   In March 2009, Georgia acceded to the Harmonized Commodity Description and Coding Systems (HS 2007); it already applied the HS 2002. The tariff classification of goods was previously based on the Foreign Economic Activity Commodity Nomenclature (FEACN).

Tariff structure

17.   The tariff comprises three bands (0%, 5% and 12%) with a maximum tariff of 12% (Table III.2). Most imported goods currently enter duty free; the higher rates apply mainly to agricultural goods and construction materials produced in Georgia (Chart lll.1). Over 98% of tariff lines have *ad valorem* rates; 183 lines are subject to specific duties, mainly on alcoholic beverages, excluding beer.

Table III.2
Georgia's tariff bands of *ad valorem rates*, 2005 and 2009

2005		2009	
Tariff rate	No. of lines	Tariff rate	No. of lines
Duty free (%)	2,757	Duty free	9,346
4	248	5%	63
5	1,828	12%	1,303
6	613		
7	1		
8	415		
10	261		
12	3,741		
14	6		
15	110		
16	6		
17	26		
18	39		
20	149		
25	86		
30	80		
Total number of *ad valorem* rates:	10,366		10,712

Note: The 2005 tariff schedule is based on HS96 nomenclature; and the 2009 schedule is based on HS02.

Source: WTO calculations, based on data provided by the Georgian authorities.

18.   Exemptions from the customs tariff include good exports; re-exports; goods in transit; imports of goods produced in a Free Industrial Zone; goods intended for official use of diplomatic representatives in Georgia; goods intended for oil and gas operations under the Law on Oil and Gas; and imports of certain tobacco products and raw materials (until 1 January 2008). Exporters using imported inputs for export production can obtain tariff exemptions on imported inputs mainly through the temporary import regime for inward processing.

Chart III.1
Distribution of MFN tariff rates, 2005 and 2009

Number of tariff lines

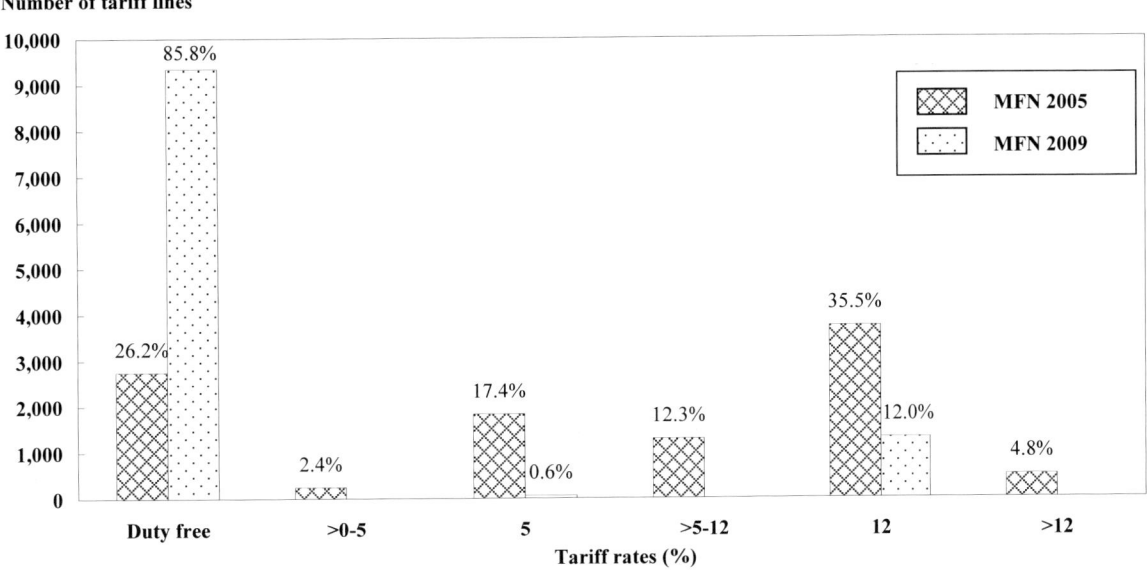

Note: Calculations exclude specific rates. Percentages denote the share of total lines. Totals do not add to 100% as no tariff rates are available for 1.5% of lines in 2005 and 1.7% in 2009 (representing specific lines).

Source: WTO Secretariat calculations, based on data provided by the Georgian authorities.

Bound MFN rates

19.   Georgia has bound all its tariffs. The average bound MFN rate is 7.5% compared with an average applied MFN rate of 1.5%, which affords only limited latitude to Georgia to raise its tariffs within existing bindings (Table III.3). The majority of tariff lines at the 12% applied rate are bound at 12% (although tobacco is bound at 30%, the highest rate). The authorities state that applied rates have not been raised during the review period.

Table III.3
Georgia's tariff structure, 2005 and 2009
(Per cent)

		MFN 2005	MFN 2009	Final bound[a]
1.	Bound tariff lines (% of all tariff lines)	100.0	100.0	100.0
2.	Simple average applied rate	7.2	1.5	7.5
	Agricultural products (HS01-24)	10.9	6.2	11.1
	Industrial products (HS25-97)	6.2	0.2	6.6
	WTO agricultural products	12.6	6.9	13.0
	WTO non-agricultural products	5.9	0.2	6.2
	ISIC 1 - Agriculture, hunting, fishing	10.0	3.6	10.0
	ISIC 2 - Mining	12.8	7.5	12.7
	ISIC 3 - Manufacturing	7.0	1.3	7.3
	First stage of processing	8.8	2.9	8.6

Table III.3 (cont'd)

		MFN 2005	MFN 2009	Final bound[a]
	Semi-processed products	5.9	0.5	6.1
	Fully processed products	7.6	1.7	8.0
3.	Tariff quotas (% of all tariff lines)	0.0	0.0	0.0
4.	Domestic tariff "peaks" (% of all tariff lines)[b]	1.6	12.5	1.8
5.	International tariff "peaks" (% of all tariff lines)[c]	3.7	0.0	3.8
6.	Overall standard deviation of tariff rates	5.8	3.9	5.8
7.	Coefficient of variation of tariff rates	0.8	2.6	0.8
8.	Duty free tariff lines (% of all tariff lines)	26.3	85.8	24.9
9.	Non-*ad valorem* tariffs (% of all tariff lines)	1.5	1.7	1.7
10.	Non-*ad valorem* tariffs with no AVEs (% of all tariff lines)	1.5	1.7	1.7
11.	Nuisance applied rates (% of all tariff lines)[d]	0.0	0.0	0.0

a   Implementation of the U.R. was achieved in 2006. Calculations for final bound rates are based on 2009 tariff schedule.

b   Domestic tariff peaks are defined as those exceeding three times the overall simple average applied rate. This includes lines at 5% and 12%.

c   International tariff peaks are defined as those exceeding 15%.

d   Nuisance rates are those greater than zero, but less than or equal to 2%.

Note: Calculations exclude specific rates (all of which are under HS Chapter 22 (alcoholic beverages)). The 2005 tariff schedule is based on HS96 nomenclature, consisting of 10,524 tariff lines; 2009 schedule is based on HS02 nomenclature, consisting of 10,895 tariff lines.

Source: WTO calculations, based on data provided by the Georgian authorities.

Applied MFN rates

20.   As noted, Georgia's current average applied MFN rate is 1.5%, down from 7.2% in 2005. Currently 86% of tariff lines are duty free compared with 26% in 2005. Above average applied rates concern live animals and products, vegetable products, prepared foods, mineral products, and articles of stone (Chart III.2). The 5% tariff rate is applied on 63 lines, consisting mainly of cheese products and certain vegetables; 1,303 tariff lines carry the 12% applied rate, the main product groups being live poultry, meat, dairy products, edible vegetables, fruits and nuts, products of the milling industry, sugar and sugar confectionary, non-alcoholic beverages and beer, salt, plastering materials, and lime and cement.

Tariff escalation

21.   There is effectively no tariff escalation nor any evident international tariff peaks.

Tariff quotas

22.   Georgia does not maintain tariff quotas.

(c)   Other charges affecting imports

23.   In addition to the customs tariff, the Georgian authorities apply VAT and excise taxes on imported goods. These taxes apply equally to domestically produced and imported goods. The authorities state that excise tax on tobacco is an exception but that the Government intends to equalize the excise tax on imported and domestically produced tobacco products. A customs fee also applies.

Chart III.2
Average applied MFN and bound rates, by HS section, 2005 and 2009

Per cent

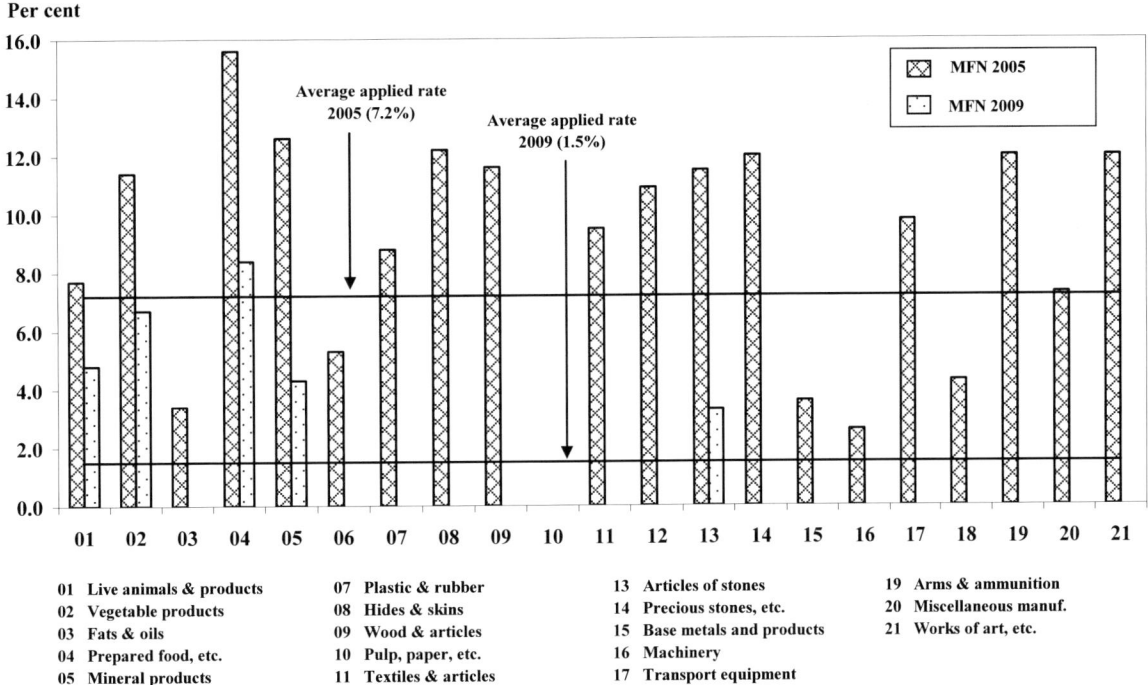

Note: Averages for 2005 are based on HS96 nomenclature, consisting of 10,524 tariff lines, and for 2009 on HS02, consisting of 10,895 tariff lines.   Exlcuding specific rates.

Source: WTO Secretariat calculations, based on data provided by the Georgian authorities.

Value-added tax

24.   The new Tax Code, effective from January 2005, reduced the rate of VAT from 20% to 18% on imported goods and services.   Exports of goods from the territory of Georgia are zero rated.   The VAT paid on imported or domestically produced inputs for export production is subject to reimbursement. In the case of imported inputs, a tax credit is given to the extent that such inputs are incorporated in the exported product;   the VAT is refunded on domestically produced inputs.

Excise tax

25.   Imports that are subject to excise duty are defined by the Tax Code of Georgia.   The number of such products has been reduced from 23 to 20, including the following goods: alcoholic drinks; condensed natural gas (except for pipeline);   oil distillates; goods produced from crude oil; tobacco products;   and automobiles.   Excisable exports are zero rated, with the exception of ferrous and non-ferrous metal scrap.   Excise tax rates are fixed per physical unit of excisable goods (litre, cm^3, kilogram, tonne, etc).

Customs fees

26.   Customs fees are payable at the time of declaration of the goods to Customs and are due on import and temporary admission.   The rates on imports are: 60 euro equivalent in GEL per declaration, and for goods with a customs value of less than GEL 3,000, 5 euro equivalent in GEL per

declaration. The fee for customs procedures related to temporary admission varies according to weight.

(iii)   Customs valuation, rules of origin, and preshipment inspection

(a)   Customs valuation

27.   Customs valuation for imported goods is administered in accordance with chapter 6 of the revised customs code. Apart from a limited number of products subject to specific duties, Customs collects duties on the c.i.f. value of the imported goods. For this purpose, the general rule is that the customs value will be the price actually paid or payable (the transaction value) for the goods when sold for export to Georgia. However, a number of additions are made to the price paid or payable if those elements have not already been included in the selling price, including: transportation costs, commissions and brokerage, loading and handling charges, warehousing charges, royalties and licence fees related to the goods being valued, insurance charges, other similar charges incurred with respect to the goods before their customs clearance. Provided that certain costs are shown separately from the price actually paid or payable, the customs value does not include: charges for the transport of goods from the Customs; buying commissions; charges for the right to reproduce imported goods in Georgia and other similar charges.

28.   When the transaction value of the imported goods cannot be used, the importer must rely on the following alternatives in the order specified below, except that the last two options can be reversed at the request of the declarant: the transaction value of identical goods; the transaction value of similar goods; the unit price of goods; the computed value; and the reserve method. The authorities note that over 90% of all goods (except cars, which are cleared according to fixed rates) are cleared using the transaction value.

(b)   Rules of origin

29.   The criteria for determining the country of origin are defined in Chapter 5 of the revised code of Georgia. For goods of non-preferential origin, Georgia adheres to WTO rules on determination of country of origin. Regarding preferential origin, Georgia issues three different types of certificate of origin: for the CIS free-trade area, in accordance with the rules of origin defined by the Decision of Council of Governments of CIS countries, 30 November 2000; for products covered by the scheme of Generalized System of Preference (GSP); and for application of the preferences provided for under the FTA between Georgia and the Republic of Turkey.

(c)   Preshipment inspection

30.   In accordance with the revised Customs Code of Georgia, effective January 2007, pre-shipment inspection has been abolished.

(iv)   Import prohibitions, restrictions, and licensing

31.   Georgia prohibits the import of goods that pose a threat to the health and safety of Georgia or its citizens, including narcotics, pornography, nuclear materials, and goods that may not be in compliance with Georgia's obligations under certain international conventions such as the Montreal Protocol and CITES. According to the authorities, Georgia has no quantitative restrictions (quotas) on trade.

32.   The import licensing system was simplified when the Georgian Parliament adopted the new Law on licences and permits in June 2005. Accordingly, the total number of business licences and

permits required was cut to 144 (92 licences and 52 permits), representing only 16% of previous requirements. Licences and permits for export/import were reduced from 14 main groups to 8, with licensing limited to protecting public health, the environment, and national security. Weapons and ammunition have complex licensing requirements, administered by the Ministries of Justice (Table III.4). Other imports requiring licensing include those subject to phytosanitary and veterinary control, materials of limited circulation, dual-purpose goods, therapeutic agents subject to special control, and endangered species of flora.

Table III.4
Overview of the import licensing system, 2009

Licensing body	Products	Objective
Ministry of Agriculture	Products of floral origin subject to phytosanitary control Products subject to veterinary control Non-iodic salt	Food safety and public health
Ministry of Environmental Protection and Natural Resources	Endangered wild flora or fauna specimens Nuclear and radioactive objects, nuclear materials, radioactive substances, radioactive wastes, minerals (subsoil) from which it is practically possible to extract nuclear materials, all that is made of nuclear materials or radioactive substances or contains them as a component, also nuclear technologies	Environmental protection
Ministry of Justice, according to the recommendation of the Permanent Commission on Military-Technical Issues of the Ministry of Defence of Georgia	Military and surveillance equipment	National security
Ministry of Health and Social Affairs of Georgia, taking into account the requirements of the existing UN Convention	Medicines and pharmaceuticals subject to special control	Public health
Ministry of Economic Development	Dual purpose products	National security

Source: WTO document G/LIC/N/3/GEO/3, 4 September 2006.

(v)   Contingency measures

33.   Georgia does not use anti-dumping, countervailing or safeguard measures, and no relevant legislative basis has been elaborated.

(vi)   Government procurement

34.   Georgia is an observer to the WTO Agreement on Government Procurement and, in principle, welcomes membership. A new Law on State Procurement (LSP) was approved in April 2005 and entered into force in January 2006, replacing the LSP of 1998. The law applies to the procurement of all goods, works, and services funded from state and local budgetary resources by about 3,500 procuring entities. Based on figures provided by the State Budget Department of the Ministry of Finance, the authorities estimate that total government procurement expenditures in 2008 amounted to 16.4% of GDP; three quarters of this was accounted for by central budget expenditures and the rest by the budgets of territorial units.[8] They also note that the participation of foreign companies was not restricted.

35.   Foreign and local companies have equal access to the Georgian procurement market. To promote the development of domestic contracting and manufacturing industries, until 2006, they were granted a 15% margin of preference in the evaluation of bids offering inputs (material and labour)

---

[8] Central budget spending in terms of GDP broke down as follows: goods and services 7.9% and non-financial activities 4.7%. Of the total number of tenders (2,791) conducted in 2008, 82% were for goods and services and the rest for construction/reconstruction works.

from Georgia when foreign and domestic bidders participate in the tender. Under the 2006 law, all such preferences were abolished. Guidelines and manuals are only available in Georgian.

36.   The regulating and monitoring body that ensures compliance with the LSP is the State Procurement Agency (SPA), which develops normative regulations and standard bidding documents and is responsible for disseminating information about procurement, including through the launching of its website (www.spa.ge). Previously under the auspices of the Ministry of Economic Development, under amendments made in 2007, the SPA is now accountable to the Prime Minister in order to avoid any conflicts of interest given that the MoED is a significant procuring entity. Legislative amendments currently before Parliament aim to: increase transparency in the procurement process by introducing electronic procurement, and establish a dispute review body to conduct independent reviews of complaints.

37.   The national threshold for small purchases is GEL 120,000 for works and GEL 50,000 for goods and services. Above these thresholds, open competition should be used, although, according to the World Bank, data on the amount of procurement and the number of contracts awarded by open competition and other methods are not available.[9] Furthermore, emergency provisions for sole sourcing (Article 10.1 of the LSP) are applied widely; the World Bank estimates that more than 50% of all signed contracts are single sourced.[10] According to the same source, the ratio of contracts procured through tenders is 12%, the remaining 88% being conducted through other (less competitive) methods, such as request for quotations and single source.[11] However, this may be changing: after the adoption of the new framework, public tenders increased from 796 in 2005 to over 3,500 in 2007 and the number is expected to rise higher as the monitoring capacity of the SPA increases. There are mechanisms to contest procurement decisions and, according to the authorities, companies found guilty of corruption in procurement processes are placed on a special list and are prohibited from participating in future bids for up to two years.

(vii)   State trading and other measures

38.   Georgia has notified the WTO that it does not maintain any state-trading enterprises in accordance with Article XVII:4(a) of the GATT 1994.[12] According to the authorities, Georgia applies no trade sanctions, other than those endorsed by the UN Security Council. It does not engage in countertrade or barter.

(3)   MEASURES DIRECTLY AFFECTING EXPORTS

(i)   Documentation

39.   Documentation requirements applying to exporters are stipulated in Order No. 1770 of the Ministry of Finance (see section (2)(i)(a)).

---

[9] World Bank-European Commission (2008), p. 27. Overall, the World Bank-EU Commission report notes that while the legislative framework is partially aligned with international practice, weaknesses remain, e.g. in over-reliance on single source procurement, and poor working of the complaint mechanism.

[10] World Bank (2008), p. 27.

[11] The Georgian authorities note that the breakdown cited is according to the number of tenders and not to the volume of business. In value terms, the biggest share of public procurement is accounted for by tenders and not by single source.

[12] WTO document G/STR/N/7GEO, 16 September 2002.

(ii)   **Export taxes, charges, and levies**

40.   In accordance with the customs legislation of Georgia, no tariff duty is applied to exports or re-exports. The VAT rate on exports is zero. Exported goods are not subject to excise duty, except for waste and scrap of ferrous and non-ferrous metals.

(iii)   **Export prohibitions, restrictions, and licensing**

41.   Georgia does not use export quotas or minimum export prices.

42.   Export licensing restrictions are applied only for reasons of healthcare, environmental protection, national heritage, and security, on: goods of cultural value (Ministry of Culture, Monument Protection and Sport); means of electronic surveillance (Ministry of the Interior); materials of limited circulation (Ministry of Environmental Protection and Natural Resources); arms and ammunition (Ministry of Defence); dual-purpose goods (Ministry of Economic Development); therapeutic agents subject to special control (Ministry of Health and Social Affairs); and endangered species of flora and fauna (Ministry of Environmental Protection and Natural Resources).

(iv)   **Export subsidies, export promotion, and export finance**

(a)   Export subsidies

43.   In accordance with its WTO commitments, Georgia does not apply any prohibited subsidies, including export subsidies, within the meaning the WTO Agreement on Subsidies and Countervailing Measures.

(b)   Export promotion and finance

44.   The authorities state that the Export Promotion Department under the MoED is responsible for providing advice to exporters on trade- and market-related issues. There is no government financing for exporters. Other than ordinary bank loans at market interest rates, no official or other financing facilities are available for exporters.

(v)   **Free industrial zones**

45.   In June 2007, Parliament adopted the Law of Georgia on Free Industrial Zones[13], which sets out the terms and conditions for establishing and operating free industrial (or economic) zones in Georgia. According to Article 1, the law aims to create an attractive climate for economic activities and to promote the inflow of capital, technology, and know-how. Financial operations in such zones can be carried out in any currency and there is a special taxation regime for companies.

46.   The law defines rules for the creation, liquidation and management of free industrial zones, and for the creation and functioning of administrative and service/supervisory bodies; it also determines additional terms and corporate tax preferences for the free industrial zone enterprises and other issues related to the functioning of the zones. In 2008, two sub-legislative acts were adopted by the Government: the Rules on Establishment, Arrangement and Operation of Free Industrial Zones (Government's Resolution #131); and the act on Determining the Amount of the Guarantee to be Submitted for Creation of Free Zones, Conditions for Creation of Free Zones, their Operation, Storage of Goods and Customs Control Rule" (Government's Resolution No. 157).

---

[13] Law on Free Industrial Zones (unofficial translation by USAID). Viewed at: http://www.georgia. gov.ge/pdf/200903272229041.pdf.

47.   The Ministry of Economic Development allocated 400 hectares adjacent to the Black Sea port of Poti for the first such zone, where construction work is under way. In 2009, the Kutaisi Free Industrial Zone was created on a 25-hectare site where the Kutaisi automotive factory was previously located.

(4)   MEASURES AFFECTING PRODUCTION AND TRADE

(i)   Legal framework for businesses

48.   The business environment in Georgia has changed substantially in recent years. Regulation of business entry has been streamlined: the number of business activities subject to licences and permits has been reduced by 84% since 2005; licensing procedures have been simplified; and the "one-stop shop" approach to business regulation has been adopted. Further, entry barriers in the form of minimum capital requirements were lowered and subsequently abolished. As regards regulation of ongoing business, operational licensing, permits, inspections, and other compliance systems, including taxes and customs, have become more business-friendly. Contract enforcement has been strengthened by reforming court procedures for commercial disputes. The new Labour Code eases restrictions on duration of contracts and overtime, and simplifies regulations on severance pay and labour dispute resolution.

(a)   Business registration

49.   In 2005, business registration procedures were simplified. Paperwork and fees were reduced, and the processing time was shortened initially to a week and now to about one day from the submission of documents. All companies are required to register with the Ministry of Finance, and must provide founders' and principals' names, dates and places of birth, occupations, and places of residence; incorporation documents; area of activity; and charter capital. This information is made public and available on request by any person. Business registration and tax registration are separate procedures handled by the same department within the Ministry of Finance.

50.   The main laws regulating business are: the Law on Entrepreneurs (1994), which defines types of legal-organizational form for enterprises, terms of registration, internal structure of the entities; the Law on Supervision on Entrepreneurship (2001), which sets general rules for supervision activity by the state controlling authorities; and the Law on Insolvency (2007), which regulates insolvency proceedings of entities. As a result of changes to the Law on entrepreneurs in 2005 and 2006, business registration is simpler and more efficient, taking only one day for legal entities and individuals; state and tax registration of companies is now carried out by tax inspectorates under a single procedure. There are no restrictions on foreign ownership of companies in Georgia. Foreign participation is allowed in: sole proprietorship, limited partnership, general partnership, cooperative, limited liability company, joint-stock company. A foreign company may also open a branch or representative office in Georgia. Most foreign investors set up limited liability companies, joint-stock companies or branch offices to do business in Georgia.

51.   Provisions regarding access to information on companies and protection of shareholder rights were also strengthened in amendments made in 2007. Auditing of financial statements of Georgian business entities is obligatory only for banks, insurance companies, companies whose stock is accepted for trade on the stock exchange, and some other businesses.

(b)   Licensing

52.   According to the Georgian authorities, a licensing and permit system is one of the most significant preconditions for ensuring the proper functioning of a liberal market economy. Generally,

the business licensing system plays a decisive role in creating a business-friendly regulatory environment that is aimed at creating jobs and supporting investments.

53.   By adopting the 2005 framework Law on Licences and Permits, the Government initiated one of the most important reforms for liberalizing the business environment and combating widespread corruption. The reform eliminated licences and permits that could not be properly explained or justified, and as a result, decreased the total number of licences and permits from 909 to 137. Two major principles were declared mandatory: the "Silence is Consent Principle"[14], and the "One Stop Shop" mechanism; these essentially changed the procedures for obtaining a licence/permit, and made them clear, transparent, and predictable.   Another major achievement of the reform was the introduction of a 30-day time limit to issue a licence and a 20-day period for a permit, thus cutting off opportunities for bribes and misuse of state authority. However, an International Finance Corporation analysis of progress in implementing the framework law notes, *inter alia,* that the "silence is consent" principle has not been fully implemented[15] (Table AIII.1). Although the framework law contains an exhaustive list of licences and permits, it lacks any indication of the corresponding issuing bodies and, coupled with frequent changes to the law, this has hampered implementation.

54.   Under the law, the following activities are subject to licensing: producing and packing baby foodstuff; producing and packing children's food; nuclear activity and activities related to nuclear materials and installations; production of biological pesticides; production, repair, and sale of weapons; production, buying, import, and export of electronic surveillance equipment; local broadcasting; producing, transferring, dispatching, and distributing electricity;   distribution and transportation of gas; oil and gas processing; transportation of oil; educational activity; insurance and re-insurance; banking; non-banking credit-deposit activity; security register activity; stock exchange; brokerage; central depositor activities; specialized depositor activities; management of assets; medical activities; mining; use of subsurface area; use of oil and gas resources; use of wood resources; keeping hunting farms; fishing; regular international air transportation; use of numeric resources; use of radio frequencies.

55.   Around 50 other types of activity, including import and export of weapons, are subject to special permission. The issuing body is required to grant a licence within 30 days after an application is filed or a permit within 20 days after an application is filed. The licence or permit is granted automatically if the administrative body does not respond to the application within the time limits. In some areas of business activity, the mandatory timeframe for issuing licences and permits is shorter.

(ii)   Incentives

(a)   Special taxation regimes

56.   According to the authorities, no specific incentives are currently envisaged under Georgian tax legislation. There are, however, special taxation regimes for international financial companies, international companies operating in a free industrial zone and for free warehouse companies (Table III.5). Under the Law on free industrial zones and the Tax Code of Georgia, companies registered and operating in free industrial zones are exempted from VAT and property tax. The import of foreign goods into free industrial zones is exempted from VAT and customs duties. The term International Financial Company (IFC) is defined in the Tax Code as a financial company receiving no more than 10% of total revenue from activities in Georgia. Under the Code, profits gained by an IFC from its financial operations are exempted from profit tax.

---

[14] Means that if a licence/permit is not issued within the timeframe set by the law, the licence/permit shall be deemed granted.

[15] International Finance Corporation (2008).

Table III.5
Special taxation regimes, 2009

Type of tax	International financial company	International company operating in a free industrial zone	Free warehouse company
Corporate income tax	0%	0%	0%
Value added tax	0%	0%	0%
Customs duties	0%, 5% or 12%	0%	0%
Property tax	up to 1%	0%	up to 1%
Personal income tax	20%	20%	20%

Source: Georgian authorities.

(b)   State aid

57.   According to the Law on Free Trade and Competition, state aid is one-time aid conferred by the Government for a definite period; it takes various forms (exemption from taxes or deferred payment, clearance of debts, restructuring, credit remittance with preferential conditions and guarantees, acquisition of immovable property with special conditions, preferential conditions during state procurement, revenue guarantees, or granting other exclusive rights).

58.   The authorities note that government economic programmes, including those aimed at industry assistance, are open and transparent and selection is on a competitive basis. The "Cheap Credit" programme, implemented in 2008, allocated GEL 62 million to 117 projects to develop activities in agriculture, food processing, handicrafts, and tourism. The number of new jobs and indirect beneficiaries from the projects exceeds 32,000 persons. The "100 New Agro Industry Enterprises" programme was launched in 2007-08 to stimulate establishment of new agricultural processing enterprises and support job creation in rural areas. Under the programme an entrepreneur may purchase state-owned land at below market price with obligation of creating processing infrastructure and employment. One of the selection criteria is the number of new jobs to be created; ten projects have been developed under the programme.

(c)   Pricing policies

59.   Policies adopted in the early 1990s had led to a broad-based liberalization of prices, and removed virtually all government administrative controls on prices for energy, transport, and other social services. Price controls had been replaced by tariff regulation by local governments or, in the case of electricity and natural gas, by independent regulatory commissions established for the purpose. Apart from price controls for natural gas, electricity, water, and urban transport, prices for all other goods and services were determined by the market. According to the Georgian authorities, price regulation is currently in place only in regulated spheres, such as the electronic communications, energy and water sectors. Prices of local (municipal) passenger transportation are regulated by the municipal authority, according to Presidential Decree No. 104.

(iii)   State-owned enterprises and privatization

60.   Since Independence, Georgia has undergone economic transition from a centrally planned to a market-based economy, with major reforms of its trade regime, services sectors, and extensive privatization of state property. The privatization programme launched in 1993 involved mostly small and medium-scale entities (commercial, household servicing establishments, retail stores, etc.). According to the authorities, from 2003 to 2008, the share of the public sector in total output declined from 32% to 10% and during the same period the number of persons in public-sector employment

declined from 47% to 26% of total employment.[16] No statistics are available on the share of imports or exports accounted for by state-owned companies although the authorities maintain that there are no export-oriented state-owned enterprises.

61.   The Government restarted the privatization process in 2004 focusing on large-scale enterprises. Between 2005 and 2008, the Government received more than US$1.4 billion in revenue from the privatization process (Chart III.3)[17], mostly from: telecommunications, energy (hydropower generation plants and energy distribution companies), large-scale real estate assets and, more recently, hospitals. In the ports and mining sectors, licenses are issued to operators.

Chart III.3
Privatized units and income from privatization, 1995-2008

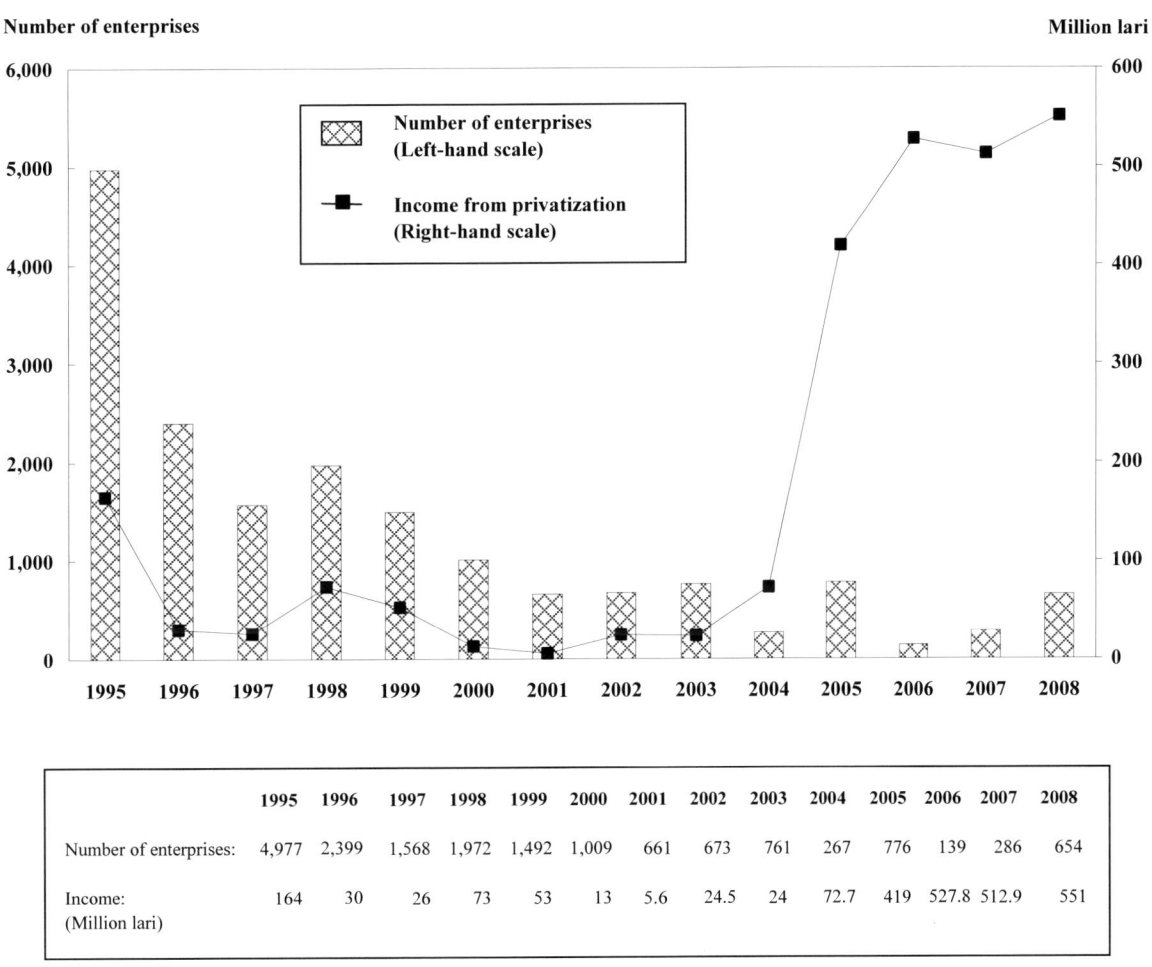

	1995	1996	1997	1998	1999	2000	2001	2002	2003	2004	2005	2006	2007	2008
Number of enterprises:	4,977	2,399	1,568	1,972	1,492	1,009	661	673	761	267	776	139	286	654
Income: (Million lari)	164	30	26	73	53	13	5.6	24.5	24	72.7	419	527.8	512.9	551

Source: UNDP, *Human Development Report 2008, 2008 data provided by the Georgian authorities.*

62.   According to the authorities, in the first seven months of 2009, a further 384 entities were privatized generating over GEL 117 million. Georgia intends to continue its policy of privatizing state-owned assets; by the end of 2009, privatized at least two thirds of the shares of the Georgian

---

[16] The Georgian public sector comprises: central government units, local governments, legal entities of public law (generally subordinated to sector ministries), and SOEs.

[17] Revenue in U.S. dollars according to the Department of Statistics: 2005: 232; 2006: 317; 2007: 385; 2008 (est.): 468; 2009 (6 months): 71.

State Electricity Company; it expects to have Georgian Post; about 100,000 hectares of agricultural land; several regional airports; and numerous other SOEs. The Government has privatized, or is in the process of privatizing, most of the largest SOEs.[18]

63.   So far, more than 15,500 enterprises have been privatized.   However, around 1,300 enterprises remain with significant government ownership, including some strategically important enterprises, according to the World Bank.[19]   SOEs are monitored, on a dividend-oriented basis, by the State Enterprise Management Agency (SEMA), which replaced the Ministry of State Property Management in 2003, and reports to the Minister of Economic Development. The state budget no longer subsidizes the SOEs.

64.   The privatization process is regulated by: the Law of Georgia on State Property Privatization (revised in 2008);   Regulations on Privatization of State Property through Auction (revised 2008); and Regulations on Privatization of State Property through the Direct Sale Method (also revised in 2008).[20]   On October 2007, the Parliament adopted amendments to the Law on Privatization of the State-Owned Agricultural Lands in order to simplify procedures regarding leased land privatization. A number of privatization methods are used: auction, tender, lease, and direct sale, and there is provision for investor-initiated privatization.

(iv)   Competition policy

65.   The basic law regulating competition policy is the Law on Free Trade and Competition adopted in June 2005, replacing the 1996 Law on Monopoly Activities and Competition.[21]   The new Law aims to protect, maintain, and stimulate competition but, in the view of some observers, its scope is limited as it does not regulate restrictive agreements, concerted practices, abuse of dominant position, or mergers. According to Transparency International Georgia, for example, the new law concerns primarily state aid to industry but does not "touch the traditional fields of competition law, such as agreements restricting competition, concerted practices, abusing dominant position in the market, takeovers and mergers, state enterprises and so called natural monopolies".[22] According to GEPLAC (the Georgian-European Policy and Legal Advice Centre), the main effect of the law has been to create "a competition-law-free country with the exception of the general prohibition of state aids or subsidies".[23]

66.   In parallel to the legislative changes, institutional restructuring led to the establishment of the Agency for Free Trade and Competition, the body charged with overseeing the law, although its powers are restricted to giving recommendations. It seems that special attention is needed to increase the institutional power, administrative capacity and the independence of the Free Trade and Competition Agency which is still a structural unit of the Ministry of Economic Development with only an advisory role; in addition, it lacks legal mechanisms to assure the enforcement of the its decisions.

---

[18] See Ministry of Economic Development online information. Viewed at: www.privatization.ge.

[19] World Bank (2008), p. 15.

[20] See Ministry of Economic Development online information. Viewed at: http//www.privatization.ge.

[21] The Law on Monopolistic Activity and Competition prohibited agreements or decisions which restrict competition, the abuse of a monopolistic position and unfair competition. The Government was also subject to a number of prohibitions, including the granting of fiscal or other privileges, which afforded economic agents advantages over their competitors, and on state monopolization which could lead to a restriction of competition.

[22] Transparency International Georgia (2008a), p. 2.

[23] Georgian Law Review (2006).

67.   As noted by some observers, the law on Free Trade and Competition is mainly focused on state aid. Any form of state aid that distorts or threatens to distort competition is prohibited, except when stipulated by the law, e.g. *force majeure*, development of certain economic activities. The Law defines state aid as any form of assistance by the Government on a one-time basis, including: tax exemption or prolongation; cancelling of debts; restructuring; granting of concessionary loan terms; favourable loan guarantees; providing special conditions for buying immovable property; preferential conditions in the process of state procurement; profitability guarantees; and the granting of other exclusive right to certain economic agents or production of certain commodities.

68.   State authorities establish the procedures for granting state aid, specifying the necessity for state aid, the forms it takes, and the beneficiaries, and submit the information to the Agency. The Agency prepares recommendations and may raise any state aid infringement issues with the Government. The Agency has the right to provide directions and recommendations to the state and local authorities when illegal decisions have been made, and in case of infringement of competition law, may raise the question of disciplinary, administrative, and criminal liability. With respect to economic agents, it has the right to require any documentation from the economic agent regarding any actions that infringe the provisions of competition law, and demand that any illegal actions be brought into conformity.

69.   Some sector-specific anti-monopoly regulations are enforced through independent national regulatory commissions in key sectors – energy, water supply, communication, transport, and financial sector. Electronic communications are regulated by the Georgian National Communications Regulatory Commission in accordance with the Law on Electronic Communications (2005, No. 1514); the financial sector (commercial banks, insurance companies) is regulated by the Financial Supervision Agency (FSA), as governed by the Law on Commercial Banks Activity (1996, No. #121); and energy and water supply is regulated by the Georgian National Energy and Water Supply Regulatory Commission, in accordance with the Law on Power Industry and Natural Gas (1997, No. #816).

70.   Regulations, and related sanctions against monopolistic activity and other violations of Georgian law are provided in the Criminal Code and Administrative Code of Georgia. According to the authorities, regulations on protection of competition are provided in several normative acts of Georgian legislation and adequately reflect a comprehensive and targeted approach to anti-monopoly regulation in specific sectors.

(v)   Standards and SPS requirements

(a)   Standards and certification

Main developments since accession

71.   During the course of its transition to a market economy, Georgia has made major changes in this area. Mandatory standards, such as the Soviet-era GOST standards, were used in the past to ensure that products conformed to the directives issued by central authorities. Upon entering the WTO, Georgia agreed to ensure that the application of these standards would be made voluntary and that they would only be mandatory if they became technical regulations adopted by a public authority in accordance with legitimate objectives such as health and safety. Georgia's acceptance of the TBT Code of Good Practice has helped to change its standardization and certification procedures by encouraging the transition to voluntary standardization as well as the application of international standards. During a transitional period, GOST and other regional standards continue to apply on a mandatory basis but only on products produced in Georgia or imported from non-WTO CIS states.

72.   In 2005, the Government carried out legislative and institutional reforms to the standards infrastructure to enable Georgia to transition to a system of voluntary standards and certification, whereby the importer may choose to align his products to Georgian standards, international standards or the standards of any EU or OECD member state. If foreign standards are chosen, they must be registered by the importer in the National Agency for Standardization, Technical Regulations and Metrology, the main standards organization. Georgia acknowledges the standards of 36 countries, whose products may enter the Georgian market without any further conformity assessment or legalization procedures; the share of these countries in Georgia's total imports amounted to around 35% in 2008.

73.   According to the principle of voluntary standardization, local entrepreneurs are free to use a variety of standards: international standards, GOSTs, and even their own standards. ISO standards are available to local producers through the Agency, which has access to the ISO standards database. Each standard applied by the producer should be registered with the Agency. The Agency also carries out the registration of international standards (mainly ISO standards) as national standards. The authorities maintain that GOST standards do not have the status of national standards, and that they are applied, mostly in the field of testing methods, because the equipment used in the manufacturing process and in testing laboratories is outdated.

74.   Adoption of new national standards – based on international and European Norms (EN) (under Article 51 of the PCA[24]) – is making progress; as of 1 July 2009, over 2,500 international (mainly ISO) and European standards had been adopted and registered as Georgian national standards (Table III.6). Of the 1,765 international standards adopted in 2008-09, 22% were on foodstuffs and agricultural products, 20% on power engineering and fuel, 14% on industry products and machinery, and 6% each on building materials and chemicals. Of the 113 European standards adopted in the same period, 64 were for building materials and 49 for industry products and machinery.

Table III.6
Georgian standards, 2006-09

Standards	2006	2007	2008	2009	Total
Georgian national standards	18	8	3	2	31
International/European standards adopted as Georgian standards	275	357	893	872	2,397[a]
Standards of foreign countries adopted as Georgian national standards, that are developed on the basis of international standards	..	12	27	..	39
Standards of foreign countries adopted as Georgian national standards	77	43	50	..	170
GOST standards	0	0	0	0	0
Total	370	420	973	874	2,637

..   Not available.

a   Of which: ISO, 1,949; EN standards, 113; Codex Alimentarius, 224; Oil products (ASTM, IP), 111.

Source: Georgia authorities.

Legal and institutional reforms

75.   Upon acceding to the WTO, Georgia committed itself to adopt a new standards system comprising voluntary standards and mandatory international technical regulations replacing the Soviet system of mandatory standards. The Law on Standardization, adopted in 1999, introduced the principle of voluntary standardization although, in practice, obsolete Soviet standards were still being

---

[24] The article states, *inter alia,* that "the required actions in quality assurance infrastructure will facilitate progress towards mutual recognition in the field of conformity assessment, as well as the improvement of the quality of Georgian products".

used. Under the 2005 reform, in order to meet the requirements of the WTO and align the system to international practice, legislative changes were made to three laws: the Law on Standardization (transposition from mandatory to voluntary standardization system, introduction of the concept of technical regulation, establishment of GEOSTM, the standards agency); the Law on Ensuring Uniformity of Measurements (simplification of system of legal measuring instruments); and the Law on Certification of Production and Services" (provision that line ministries and other state authorities use respective EU directives to elaborate technical regulations, abolition of list of products and services subject to mandatory certification, creation of national accreditation body, and establishment of unified national system for approving competence of conformity assessment bodies).

76.   Until 2005, the main standardization body was Sakstandardi, the State Department for Standardisation, Certification and Metrology. All goods and products produced in, imported into or exported from Georgia had to meet Georgian standards and receive certification from Sakstandarti. In 2005, its metrology, accreditation, certification, and market supervision functions were restructured between two separate legal entities (of public law) under the Ministry of Economic Development of Georgia: the Georgian National Agency for Standards, Technical Regulations and Metrology (GEOSTM), and the Georgian National Accreditation Centre.

77.   GEOSTM is divided into the Institute of Metrology, which develops and maintains standards and related reference materials, and the Department for Standards and Technical Regulations, which is responsible for registration of standards and maintenance of the register of standards. Among its functions, GEOSTM ensures the availability of international and European standards for all interested parties, is responsible for the WTO TBT enquiry point, and represents Georgia in various international and regional organizations in the field of standardization and metrology. It became a corresponding member of the ISO (International Standardization Organization) in 2006, and an associate member of CEN (European Committee for Standardization) in 2008, from which it has received full versions of all European standards.

78.   The National Accreditation Centre accredits private laboratories to conduct testing; certification is performed by accredited bodies primarily in the private sector; and market supervision is by the national service for food safety, veterinary and plant protection, and by the Georgian State Inspection for Technical Supervision.

(b)   Sanitary and phytosanitary measures

79.   According to the authorities, Georgia's sanitary and phytosanitary standards are intended solely to protect the health of human, animal, and plant life, and not to create technical barriers to trade or to protect domestic producers. In order to prepare for accession to the WTO, Georgia had revised its quarantine requirements and adopted new legislation, including the Law on protection of plants from harmful organisms (1994), the Law on agricultural quarantine (1997), and a veterinary law reflecting the standards established by the World Organisation for Animal Health (OIE). A Presidential Decree on SPS Measures was drafted to meet the requirements of the SPS Agreement, and issued in 1999.[25]

---

[25] The decree provides for observance of the requirements of the SPS Agreement, which includes: the establishment of the SPS Enquiry Point (notified officially to WTO in 1999); that SPS measures to be applied only to the extent necessary to protect human, animal, or plant health, and be based on scientific principles and supported by adequate scientific evidence; that SPS measures should be based on international standards; that they be based on risk assessments, and that they should not discriminate unjustifiably between countries; that SPS measures of countries exporting products to Georgia be accepted as equivalent, even when different from SPS measures adopted in Georgia, when the exporting country can demonstrate that its SPS measures achieve

80. Georgia is a member of, *inter alia,* the Food and Agriculture Organization (FAO), the World Health Organization (WHO), the World Organisation for Animal Health (OIE), the International Plant Protection Convention (IPPC) since 2006, and has been a member of the joint FAO/WHO Food Standards Programme-Codex Alimentarius Commission since 1998.

81. An important SPS-related legislative development occurred in 2005 when Georgia adopted a new law on "Food Safety and Quality"[26] which, unlike the former Soviet GOST food safety system, emphasizes controlling the production process rather than only end-product testing. Central to the new law is the OECD-based Hazard Analysis and Critical Control Points (HACCP) food safety system, which consists of checks at all stages of the food production and packaging process. However, due to lack of funding, insufficient institutional capacity, and fear of factory closures in the food industry because of financial inability to meet the legal requirements, the law was amended twice (in 2006 and 2007), resulting in the suspension of its core articles; according to the authorities, these will be reinstated gradually between 2010 and 2012. According to Transparency International Georgia, the country now "effectively has no legislation governing food safety because of institutional incapacity and the food industry itself is either incapable of or has no incentive to adhere to it".[27]

82. Until 2006, compliance with Georgia's regulations was determined by the State Sanitary Service and Department of Hygiene under the Ministry of Health and Social Affairs; the Sanitary, Quarantine and Supervision Department of the State Inspection on Plant Quarantine; and the Veterinary Department under the Ministry of Agriculture and Food. As part of a broader regulatory reform of agriculture, in 2006 the regulatory bodies were consolidated into a single structure called the National Service (NS) of Food Safety, Veterinary and Plant Protection (in the Ministry of Agriculture), which is responsible for food safety supervision and control. The Ministry of Health and Social Affairs sets food safety parameters and norms, and the MoF's Revenue Service is responsible for SPS border controls, where officials performing SPS controls are hired by the Customs Department.

83. The National Service of Food Safety, Veterinary and Plant Protection is responsible for inspections and controls. However, consecutive amendments to the Food Safety Law have deferred the start of inspections to the end of 2009 or beyond. The NS is due to become fully functional from January 2010, when it will have sole responsibility for food safety, excluding border controls.

84. Prior to 2006, the State Border Veterinary Supervision Inspection checked all imports of live animals, meat, and fish; animal and fish products; animal fodder and feed supplements; and veterinary preparations. A licence from the State Inspection of Plant Quarantine was required for import, re-export or transit of goods covered by plant quarantine regulations.

85. Traded goods covered by quarantine regulations include agricultural products, timber, seeds and seedlings, plants and plant parts, and plant products that could carry infectious diseases; hides and unprocessed wool; mushrooms, bacteria, viruses, nematodes, and insects on living cultures; collections of insects, which could bring plant diseases; herbaria and seed collections; agricultural

---

the same or a higher level of protection; that compliance measures be consistent with the SPS Agreement, and for a right of judicial review of administrative decisions in this area.

[26] According to the authorities, all normative acts regarding food safety were elaborated on the basis of EU regulations and notably: EC Regulation No. 178/2002 on the general principles and requirements of food law, establishing the European Food Safety Authority and laying down procedures in matters of food safety; EC Regulations Nos. 852 and 853/2004 on the hygiene of foodstuffs; and EC Regulation No. 882/2004 on official controls performed to ensure the verification of compliance with feed and food law, animal health and animal welfare rules.

[27] Transparency International Georgia (2008c).

machinery, aggregates for land development, vehicles, vessels, packaging materials, and industrial plants; and soil samples that could carry plant diseases. Imports of commodities of plant origin and other items subject to quarantine require a phytosanitary certificate issued by the quarantine service of the exporting country, as well as a certificate on the condition of the commodity, delivered by the relevant division of Georgia's Ministry of Food and Agriculture. Infested or infected shipments that cannot be disinfected are returned to the country of origin or destroyed with the owner's consent.

86.   Currently, responsibility for SPS controls at the territorial borders and ports rests solely with the Customs Department, based on rules defined by the Ministry of Agriculture. The 2007 Customs Law regulates phytosanitary and veterinary border-quarantine control with the aim of ensuring efficiency of quarantine control at Customs checkpoints. Customs, *inter alia,* carries out documentary checking and examination of imported cargos subject to quarantine regulations.

87.   Georgia's SPS system is not compatible with the EU, and this restricts the capabilities of the Georgian food industry to export its products to the EU market. Only products that do not require official health certification and for which the exporting industries in Georgia can ensure conformity with EU food safety criteria are currently exported to the EU; most important are wine and hazelnuts (where the producer can prove conformity). In order to comply with EU regulations on imports of food products of animal origin[28], Georgia is preparing to introduce a system for the approval and licensing of slaughterhouses, dairies, meat cutting plants, etc. Lack of official controls and inspections poses significant health risks for humans, animals, and plants in Georgia and countries importing Georgian agricultural products. The 2007 outbreak of African swine fever, which revealed inadequate Government response capacity, is an example of Georgia's vulnerability regarding animal health safety.

(vi)   Intellectual property rights

(a)   Overview

88.   Georgia acceded to the WTO and the TRIPS Agreement in 2000; it did not negotiate transitional period. Georgia has joined a full range of international conventions: it is a member of WIPO and a party to the Paris Convention for the Protection of Industrial Property (1994); the Patent Cooperation Treaty (1994); the Berne Convention for the Protection of Literary and Artistic Works (1995); and the Protocol Relating to the Madrid Agreement Concerning the International Registration of Marks (1998). In 2004, the Georgian Parliament ratified the Rome Convention for the Protection of the Rights of Performers, Producers of Phonograms and Broadcasting Organizations, and the Lisbon Agreement on Denominations of Origin. Georgia has been a member of the UPOV Convention for the Protection of New Varieties of Plants since November 2008. It is also a member of the WIPO Copyright Treaty and the Performance and Phonograms Treaty, the Hague Agreement, and the Nice Agreement on the International Classification of Goods and Services for the Purpose of Registration of Marks (2003). Georgia is under obligation in the Partnership and Cooperation Agreement (PCA) with the EC to provide IPR protection at a level similar to that of the Community.[29]

---

[28] Two regulations are particularly relevant: Regulation 178/2002/EC (regarding parts of animals and plants or plant products identification and traceability systems; hygiene in food processing) and "General Guidance for third country authorities on the procedures to be followed when importing live animals and animal products into the European Union", DG SANCO/FVO, October 2003 (EU requirements on animal health and the processing of animal products).

[29] Article 42 of the PCA states that "Georgia shall continue to improve the protection of intellectual, industrial and commercial property rights in order to provide, by the end of the fifth year after entry into force of this Agreement, for the level of protection similar to that existing in the Community, including effective means

The authorities state that Georgian legislation regarding copyright, geographical indications and trade marks is harmonized with EU standards and requirements and draft amendments have been prepared with respect to the protection of industrial designs and patents.

89.   The implementing agency for policy formulation and implementation is the Georgian National Intellectual Property Centre (Sakpatenti). Initially founded as a patent office, it acts as an industrial property office, a copyright office, and an agency for the protection of new plant varieties and breeder rights, which means that it deals with all intellectual property areas.[30] Sakpatenti has responsibility for WTO compliance on legislative issues. Responsibility for enforcement of IP rights is shared between the Ministry of Interior, the financial police and the Customs Department of the Ministry of Finance for enforcement at Georgia's borders. The Customs Department has developed Register to assist in identifying counterfeit goods at the border; up to 60 intellectual property objects have been registered and relevant information is published online.[31]

90.   The European Neighbourhood Policy (ENP) Action Plan is an important driver of progress in the IP field. The main priorities are to: ensure full conformity of IPR legislation with PCA obligations and TRIPS requirements and its efficient enforcement; ensure proper functioning of the judicial system to guarantee access to justice for right-holders, and availability and effective implementation of sanctions; consolidate the relevant institutional structures, as well as of the offices for industrial property rights, copyright protection, and collecting societies; extend cooperation with third-country authorities and industry associations; establish an effective system of protection for geographical indications; take measures to increase public awareness of intellectual and industrial property protection; establish an efficient system for use of patent information for enterprises and improve enforcement of the relevant conventions provided for by PCA Article 42(2).

(b)   IPR legislation

Law on patents

91.   Under the 1999 Patent Law, Sakpatenti grants patents for inventions that are considered novel, involve an inventive step, and are industrially applicable. The term of protection is 20 years from the date of filing of the application. The patent owner has the exclusive right to use or dispose of an invention at his discretion, to make a product protected by the patent, to place the object in commerce, and to derive income from its use. The patent owner can sell or otherwise alienate a patent, or grant a licence. Non-exclusive compulsory licences can be granted after 4 years of patent issuance upon the request of any interested persons (Article 61), provided that the proposed user has made efforts to obtain a licence from the right holder on reasonable terms. The law also protects inventions for 20 years, utility models for 8 years, and industrial designs for 15 years from the date of filing of the patent application.

92.   For further harmonization of Georgian IPR legislation with EU standards, Sakpatenti is currently drafting amendments to the law on patents, concerning in particular lengthening the protection of utility models to 10 years, extension of patent protection by 5 years for pharmaceutical

---

of enforcing such rights". *Official Journal of the European Communities* (1999) L 205/3. Viewed at: http://eur-lex.europa.eu/LexUriServ/LexUriServ.do?uri=OJ:L:1999:205:0003:0038:EN:PDF.

    [30] Previously Sakpatenti was responsible for matters involving industrial property rights, layout designs of integrated circuits, and appellations of origin. The Copyright Agency dealt with copyrights and neighbouring rights, and the Ministry of Agriculture was responsible for plant variety protection. The Cultural Department within the Ministry of Foreign Affairs was responsible for copyrights on literary, artistic, musical, photographic, and audiovisual works.

    [31] Ministry of Finance online information. Viewed at: www.mof.ge.

products, and streamlined procedures related to granting rights, expertise and opposition. In addition, work is under way on the preparation of a separate draft law on industrial designs, hitherto regulated by the patent law.

Law on trademarks

93.   The 1999 law defines a trade mark as a sign or a combination of signs that can be expressed graphically and is capable of distinguishing the goods and/or services of one enterprise from those of another.   Trade marks are protected through registration with Sakpatenti.   The substantive examination of a trade mark should be effected within eight months from the date of filing with Sakpatenti. Decisions on registration can be challenged in the Chamber of Appeal, and the decision of the Chamber can be appealed before a court.

94.   Registration does not depend on use, but a trade mark registration can be cancelled after five years of continuous non-use in Georgia. Service marks are protected in the same way as trade marks, and Georgian legislation protects well-known marks. A trade mark certificate is valid for an initial term of ten years from the date of registration, and can be renewed indefinitely for additional periods of ten years.   Agreements to transfer or licence a trade mark must be registered with Sakpatenti to have juridical force. Amendments to the Law on trademarks, in 2005, strengthened enforcement procedures, helped to combat production and distribution of counterfeit goods, and harmonized legislation with the relevant EC Council Directive on trade marks. It implemented the recommendations of the Caucasian Brand Protection Group on legal practice in anti-counterfeiting measures.

Law on copyrights and neighbouring rights

95.   Georgia provides copyright protection under the Civil Code, supplemented by the 1999 law on copyright and neighbouring rights, which according to the authorities, was based on the WIPO model law. In case of conflict, the provisions of the copyright law prevail.

96.   Under Article 1017, the Civil Code protects the moral and economic rights of authors, and neighbouring rights connected with performers, producers of phonograms, and broadcasting organizations. The term of protection begins from the moment of creation of the work and lasts 50 years beyond the death of the author according to the Civil Code. Copyrightable material is defined as: (i) literary works (books, brochures, articles, computer programs, etc); (ii) drama or musical-dramatic works, choreographic, mime, and other theatrical works; (iii) musical works, with or without text; (iv) audio-visual works; (v) sculptures, paintings, and architectural, graphic, lithographic, and other work of visual art; (vi) pieces of decorative-applied and monumental art; (vii) pieces of theatrical-decorative art; (viii) photographic works, and works created by means analogous to photography; (ix) maps, plans, sketches, illustrations, and other three-dimensional works belonging to geography, photography or other sciences; (x) derivative works; and (xi) collection of works or data representing results of intellectual creative activity.

97.   There are specific provisions on economic rights, rights of producers of phonograms, rights of producers of videograms, the distribution of phonogram and videograms, and rights of broadcasting organizations, as well as certain provisions on rental rights in respect of computer programs, cinematographic works, and phonograms. A court can order confiscation of copies of counterfeit works and phonograms, and the materials and equipment needed for their reproduction, which would be handed over to the right-holder or destroyed. Counterfeit copies of works and phonograms, obtained by third parties in good faith, are not subject to confiscation.

98.   Amendments to the Law on Copyright and Neighbouring Rights, adopted in June 2005, introduced and updated terminology in line with the WIPO Copyright Treaty and the Performance and Phonograms Treaty, regulated copyright and neighbouring rights on the Internet, the intellectual rights of authors of audio-visual works, intellectual right protection of databases, rules on collecting societies, and lending rights. These changes brought the Georgian copyright law into line with a number of EU Directives.[32]

Law on appellations of origin and geographical indications

99.   The 1999 Law on the protection of appellations of origin and geographical indications is based on Articles 22 to 24 of the TRIPS Agreement, and European Communities Council Regulation (EC) No. 2081/92 of 14 July 1992. In a related matter, Georgia is negotiating an agreement with the EU on the protection of geographical indications of agricultural products and foodstuffs.

Law on topographies of integrated circuits

100.   The Law on Topographies of Integrated Circuits was enacted by Parliament in June 1999.

Law on IP-related border measures

101.   The law provides for measures to prevent the import and export of goods infringing copyrights or trade marks protected under Georgian law, specifically that goods infringing copyright on trademark could, upon order of the court based on an application of the copyright or trade mark holder, be detained for up to ten days. Within that time the right holder needs to initiate proceedings on the merits against the alleged infringer. The law was prepared specifically to implement Articles 50-60 of the TRIPS Agreement. A number of amendments to the law were made in 2005 to better meet TRIPs requirements, including introduction of *ex officio* procedures and suspension procedures and establishment of a product registry.

Other matters

102.   Parallel imports are not prohibited in Georgia. There is no specific law on trade secrets. Under Article 1105 of the Civil Code, an entrepreneur who possesses a trade secret (know-how), which consists of technological, organizational or commercial information of extraordinary importance that justifies the taking of necessary and adequate measures for keeping it secret, has the exclusive right to this information. At present there is no express provision in Georgian legislation protecting test data for pharmaceuticals and agricultural chemicals.

(c)   Implementation

103.   The 1999 Code of Civil Procedure stipulates that intellectual property cases are under the jurisdiction of district/city courts, which can order a party to desist from an infringement. The Law on Trademarks allows a trade mark owner to file a civil suit seeking cessation of infringing activities, destruction of all materials carrying an infringing trade mark, and damages. The infringer could also be fined or imprisoned. The patent law and the copyright law provide equivalent protection to patent and copyright owners. Similar protection is provided by the laws on geographical indications and on

---

[32] On the legal protection of computer programs (91/250/EEC); on rental right and lending right and on certain rights related to copyright (92/100/EEC); on the term of protection of copyright and certain related rights (93/98/EEC and 2001/29/EC); on the resale right for the benefit of the author of an original work of art (2001/84/EC); on copyright applicable to satellite broadcasting and cable retransmission (93/83/EEC); and on the legal protection of databases (96/9/EC).

topographies of integrated circuits. The Criminal Code stipulates criminal penalties with respect to violation of intellectual property rights, restriction of monopolistic activities and competition, misappropriation of trade marks, including well-known trade marks, false advertising, and illegal provision or distribution of information containing commercial or banking secrets. Penalties range from a fine of GEL 500 and between six months and two years' imprisonment.

104. However, despite the body of protective legislation, actual enforcement of intellectual and industrial property rights in Georgia remains weak, thus creating little incentive for foreign companies to enter the Georgian market. This is especially true in the areas of computer software and audio- and video-tapes. According to anecdotal evidence, the circulation of counterfeit goods is widespread on Georgian markets, use of unlicensed software has been common in government offices and businesses, and internet service providers host websites loaded with unlicensed content. Nevertheless, the authorities say that the situation has improved in recent years with government offices and certain private-sector businesses (like banking) now using more licensed software.

105. There is a generally acknowledged lack of capacity in law-enforcement bodies and the judiciary system to deal with IPR infringements, which is not uncommon for post-Soviet (and many developing) countries. There is no special IPR unit in the police and there is a lack of coordination among the different enforcement agencies. The authorities do not have ex officio powers to enforce IPR protection, except for Customs regarding IP objects in the Customs Register. A lack of data makes it difficult to assess the volume of pirated and counterfeit products in circulation in Georgia, although the Government, with the assistance of UNDP, is carrying out a study.

IV.   TRADE POLICIES BY SECTOR

(1)   SECTOR OVERVIEW

1.   At Independence, shares of agriculture, industry, and services in GDP were more or less evenly split. The share of agriculture has since declined significantly, to an estimated 10.3% of GDP in 2008, although the sector remains critical for the Georgian economy with over half the labour force depending on agriculture for their livelihood.   While agriculture accounts for 18% of exports, Georgia's net trade in agriculture and food products remains negative.

2.   During the review period, real agricultural output declined by 1% whereas overall GDP growth averaged 9.7% between 2003 and 2007, led by a number of sectors, including trade services, construction, financial intermediation and manufacturing.   According to the World Bank, productivity, measured in terms of value added per employee, has improved in industrial and service sectors but not in agriculture, which accumulated an excessive labour force while showing a stagnant growth pattern (Table IV.1).   The Government and the international donor community have devoted considerable resources and efforts to improve productivity in agriculture, but the benefits have so far been negligible on overall productivity, for which Georgian data appears to be lacking.

Table IV.1
Real value added per employee[a], 1998 and 2003-07
(GEL '000)

	1998	2003	2004	2005	2006	2007
Agriculture	1.6	1.7	1.7	1.8	1.6	1.7
Services	3.3	6.5	7.5	9.1	12.0	15.8
Industry	6.2	13.6	15.1	17.0	19.0	22.2

a   Value added figure based on national accounts.

Source: World Bank (2009), *Georgia Poverty Assessment*, p. 27.   Viewed at: http://www-wds.worldbank.org/external/default/WDSContentServer/WDSP/IB/2009/04/29/000350881_20090429111740/Rendered/PDF/444000ESW0P1071C0Disclosed041281091.pdf.

3.   Among the reasons for agriculture's decline are: a shortage of credit, which has prevented farmers from purchasing high-quality seeds and fertilizers, and the small size of land plots, which prevents economies of scale and discourages mechanization.   According to the latest World Bank study, rural areas account for 59% of the total poor and 62% of the extreme poor in the country.[1] With a widening rural-urban income gap, agriculture's performance is critical for reducing poverty, which continues to be prevalent in rural areas left behind by the economic growth of recent years.   To reduce poverty in the longer term, the report recommends the introduction of measures to revitalize the agriculture sector where livelihoods continue to rely on low-productivity subsistence agriculture.

4.   Industry, comprising mining, manufacturing, utilities and construction, contributed 21.7% of GDP in 2008 and provided 10.5% of the total employed labour force in 2007. Agri-processing and energy are the most significant industries.   Construction work on two international pipelines contributed to significant expansion in the construction, industrial, and services sectors in the early 2000s. The principal minerals extracted are manganese ore, petroleum, and coal, but reserves of high-grade manganese ore are largely depleted. There are also deposits of copper, gold, and silver.

5.   Before 2004, electricity blackouts were common throughout the country, but since late 2005, distribution has been much more reliable, approaching consistent 24-hour service.   Improvements

---

[1] World Bank (2009b), p. 52.

have resulted from increased metering, better billing and collection practices, reduced theft, and management reforms. Investments have also been made in infrastructure. Through conservation, new hydroelectricity sources, and the availability of new sources of natural gas in Azerbaijan, Georgia's independence in energy supplies is increasing.

6.   The services sector has grown rapidly, accounting for over 69% of GDP in 2008, up from 56% in 2002, and engaging over one-third of the employed labour force in 2008; trade, transport, and financial services have been the main contributions. Transport is a key sector for Georgia, which is the shortest transit link from Azerbaijan and Central Asia to Europe. It also serves as a north-south transport link between the Russian Federation and Turkey and, via Armenia, to Iran. Georgia is staking its future on the revival of the ancient Silk Road as the Eurasian energy transportation corridor and as a bridge for transit of goods between Europe and Asia.

(2)   AGRICULTURE

(i)   Sector developments

7.   During the review period, the agriculture sector has failed to benefit directly from Georgia's otherwise impressive economy-wide growth, with real GDP falling by 1% between 2003 and 2007, and with considerable volatility in growth from year to year due mainly to adverse weather conditions in 2004 and 2006), exacerbated in 2006 by the effect on production of the Russian trade embargo (Table IV.2). According to the World Bank, in the decade up to 2007, real agricultural GDP increased by only 2.5%, compared with an 89% increase in real overall GDP.[2] The structure of agricultural production has also changed relatively little, with the shares of crop production and of livestock production staying relatively stable, and the composition of crop production also remaining relatively stable. The World Bank noted that: "this stable pattern of production, with the emphasis on food and forage crops, is typical of subsistence agriculture".[3]

8.   With an initially sharp decline in exports, Georgia became a large net importer of food and beverages in the early to mid 1990s and, with the combination of stagnant agricultural production and rising domestic demand for food products, food imports have continued to increase. Exports have also grown relatively rapidly but were adversely affected by the impact of the Russian trade embargo on wine, spirits and mineral water in 2006. From 2005 to 2006, beverages and spirit exports fell by 27% from US$164 million to under US$120 million. The Russian ban on these major export commodities particularly affected the wine industry; export revenues fell, and the grape cultivating industry suffered as sales prices dropped significantly. Since then, Georgian winemakers, with Government support[4], have taken steps to diversify exports, improve production quality, and reduce dependence on the Russian market. The loss of Russia as the main export market for Georgian agricultural products (80% of Georgian wine was sold there) had a negative effect on local exporters, but Georgian wine producers are intensively trying to enter new markets, mainly in east and west Europe, the CIS, the United States, and China. The situation is similar with regard to vegetables and fruits.

9.   In the FSU, Georgia was a major producer and source for a wide variety of foods and beverages. Since Independence, production of high-value tea, citrus, and grape crops, which were once the basis of Georgian agriculture, is still only a fraction of pre-independence output; only grapes and citrus have shown signs of recovery (Table IV.3).

---

[2] World Bank (2009b), p. 54.
[3] World Bank (2009b), p. 54.
[4] In the 2008 budget, GEL 600,000 were assigned to measures to promote the development of Georgian wineries, and GEL 150,000 were allocated to improving the quality control system for alcoholic beverages.

Table IV.2

Trends in agricultural performance, selected indicators, 2003-08

(Per cent and US$)

	2003	2004	2005	2006	2007	2008
National and agricultural output						
Real GDP % change (annual)	11.1	5.9	9.6	9.4	12.3	2.1
Real agricultural GDP % change (annual)	10.3	-7.9	12.0	-11.7	3.3	-2.1
Composition of agricultural output (%)						
Livestock production	47.3	50.2	47.2	57.1	44.9	51.6
Crop production	50.8	48.0	51.0	41.3	53.7	46.0
Agricultural services	1.8	1.9	1.8	1.5	1.4	2.4
Crop composition (% area)						
Cereals and pulses	66.0	66.6	65.8	68.9	69.3	..
Potatoes	6.7	7.2	7.5	7.1	7.2	..
Vegetables	8.8	9.1	10.0	10.0	12.6	..
Industrial crops	8.6	7.4	7.3	8.6	7.6	..
Forage crops	9.8	9.7	9.4	5.4	3.2	..
Agricultural trade (US$ million)						
Total imports	208.8	390.6	437.5	606.3	832.5	942.5
Food imports	124.7	214.0	237.1	343.2	491.0	..
Total exports	164.7	202.4	303.9	234.9	298.6	250.5
Food exports	65.2	89.1	123.4	102.2	134.5	..
Beverage and spirits	88.6	101.3	164.4	119.6	143.4	138.4

.. Not available.

Source: Government of Georgia (2005), (2007) and (2009), Statistical yearbook.

Table IV.3

Trends in perennial crop production, selected years

('000 tonnes)

	1990	1997	2000	2003	2007
Tea	501.7	33.2	24.0	25.5	7.5
Citrus	283.1	57.1	40.0	59.2	98.9
Grapes	691.0	309.1	210.0	200.0	227.3

Source: Government of Georgia (2005), (2007) and (2009), Statistical yearbook.

(ii)   Main structural features

10.   Georgia has favourable production conditions for a variety of annual and perennial crops, and agriculture has traditionally been one of the most significant sectors in the Georgian economy. Among the most developed agricultural sub-sectors are viticulture, tea, citrus fruits, vegetables, horticulture, and tobacco; and stock breeding includes cattle, pigs, sheep, and poultry. However, the sector presently accounts for under 10% of GDP, down from over 30% in 1990, but employs more than half of the country's labour force; in 1990 this share was only 25%.

11.   Far-reaching structural changes have occurred in Georgian agriculture since independence. In the Soviet era, large farms using plantation-style labour produced most basic crops for consumption and industry (grains, oilseeds, tea, and fruits and vegetables). Small household lots produced much of the livestock products and family subsistence and some surplus for sale in the cities. Under the land reform programme begun in 1992, the large collective farms were phased out and over one million

small farms created with an average size of under one hectare. Such household plots now account for the bulk of national production of most cereals, fruits, and vegetables. While the distribution of land for subsistence is credited with averting a collapse of rural living standards following the break-up of the FSU, the small and fragmented land plots have since become a constraint to raising rural productivity and to developing a functioning land market.

12.   Deeply rooted supply-side constraints severely hamper the ability of the small family farms that now occupy 85% of arable agricultural land to raise output in response to increased domestic and foreign demand. Small farm sizes and limited access to credit for farm inputs and investment severely limit the resources to which producers have access.[5] The reasons include small farmers' inadequate use of improved crop varieties and new technologies necessary for intensifying and diversifying production, poor quality of agricultural inputs such as fertilizers, low rate of machinery use, and limited market access. On the other hand, according to the authorities, the majority of irrigation system channels have been renewed and repaired thanks to a GEL 16.2 million allocation under the State Budget. Georgian banks have been reluctant to issue loans to farmers because of the risks associated with farming, and insurance companies still do not insure crops. Thus farmers are unable to purchase agricultural machinery, and renting services are not developed. Commercial banks are reluctant to lend to small farmers as they are considered high risk and, as a result, farmers lack working capital and resources for making on-farm investments to raise productivity. However, the "Cheap Credit" programme, launched in 2008, has helped to improve access to credit for small and medium-size operators in agriculture and agri-business.

(iii)   Government policies

13.   In the Ministry of Agriculture's Agricultural Development Strategy 2009-2011, the main goals are defined as: increasing incomes in the agricultural and food sector; providing food security for the country; and eliminating poverty in the rural areas. To achieve these aims, several priorities have been identified in the areas of food safety and quality, veterinary and plant protection, mechanization, upgrading of the processing industry, increasing soil productivity, and conservation and bio-farming. This is expected to contribute over the medium term to an enabling environment for agri-businesses and enhanced competitiveness of Georgian agricultural products in international markets. However, the State budget expenditure for agriculture and forestry is low (only 0.5% of GDP in 2006). As a result, activities that are known to have high returns to investment remain under-funded (for example agricultural research and extension). Key policies carried out during the review period include land reform, privatization of farms and agri-industry, facilitating access to finance, attracting investment, and open trade policies.

(a)   Land reform and privatization

14.   Until 2005, the State held legal title to all agricultural land. Farmers leased land from the State, which prevented them from using land as collateral against loans to expand their operations. A law on privatization of state-owned agricultural land was passed in July 2005 allowing 360,000 ha of agricultural land that was still state owned to be privatized in plots of no less than 3 ha. The objective was to promote economically viable land plots for farming and facilitate the development of a land market. So far, only about 25% of privatized arable agricultural land and around 30% of state-owned land is leased out. A new stage in the privatization of agricultural lands is under way; private ownership of land remains fragmented and the average size of private farms remains very small.

---

[5] Agriculture, by far the single biggest employer in the Georgian economy, only attracted 0.8% of total FDI in 2007 and 0.5% in 2008.

(b)   Financing

15.   In 2008, the Cheap Credit programme was launched with the aim of promoting SME development by improving access to credit resources for small and medium-sized enterprises involved in agriculture (as well as handicrafts and tourism). The credits are issued on concessional terms (lower interest rates, longer maturity and grace periods). The programme was allocated about GEL 64 million in 2008, from which GEL 27.6 million were issued to 37 companies operating in the agriculture sector; the authorities estimate approximately 25,800 direct and indirect beneficiaries in the agricultural sector. The programme has continued in 2009 financed with GEL 20 million allocated from the State Budget.

(c)   Attracting investment

16.   Taxation is one of the main determining factors of the quality of the business environment and has a significant influence on the performance of agri-business. To this end, important steps have been made to liberalize the taxation system. Property taxes have been abolished on plots of land less than 5 ha. The new Tax Code also provides for the abolition of tax on transactions in property, 0% profit tax and 0% VAT; 0% VAT on primary supply of agricultural products; and 0% import duty on agricultural and other equipment.

17.   In 2007, the Government launched a national programme – 100 New Agro-Industry Enterprises – to stimulate the establishment of new agri-processing enterprises and support job creation in rural areas. Under the scheme, an entrepreneur can purchase state-owned agricultural land at concessional prices with the obligation to create processing infrastructure and employment. The authorities note that four projects have been developed under the programme with total investment of over GEL 15 million, a little over half of which is foreign investment.

(d)   Trade policies in agricultural products

18.   Imports of agricultural products are subject only to tariffs (zero, 5% or 12%) and sanitary and phytosanitary measures. All agricultural lines are bound, and Georgia has quite low tariff rates on most agricultural products, exception of sugars and confectionary, beverages, and tobacco (Table IV.4). There is no special export regime applicable to agricultural goods, no export credits other than those available from commercial banks, and no system of export credit guarantees or insurance arranged by the Government. Georgia bound its agricultural export subsidies at zero when it acceded to the WTO, and there are no export subsidy measures in place.

19.   Georgia has adopted a number of laws covering food safety, veterinary and plant protection matters. The authorities maintain that minimum international standards for food safety have been satisfied at the legislative level and that the Government is in the process of elaborating a comprehensive food safety strategy in line with EU standards. Challenges that need to be met include the gap between the quality of inspection and testing and the requirements of international standards, the organization and responsibilities of inspection bodies and laboratories, the risks for consumers due to food-borne diseases, and the lack of slaughterhouses, which undermines food safety and meat production.

Table IV.4
Tariffs by agricultural product group, 2009
(Per cent)

	2009 MFN applied rate			Bound rates		
	Average rate	Maximum rate	Duty free lines	Average rate	Maximum rate	Duty free lines
WTO agricultural products	**6.9**	**12.0**	**37.1**	**13.0**	**30.0**	**6.5**
Animals and products thereof	9.8	12.0	17.7	11.6	12.0	3.2
Dairy products	5.5	12.0	37.5	12.6	25.0	0.0
Fruits, vegetables, plants	10.3	12.0	13.1	15.4	30.0	0.0
Coffee, tea	0.5	12.0	95.9	11.5	20.0	0.0
Cereals and preparations[a]	7.5	12.0	36.9	14.0	25.0	0.9
Oilseeds, fats and oils	0.0	0.0	100.0	3.0	12.0	73.0
Sugars and confectionary	11.3	12.0	4.3	11.7	12.0	0.0
Beverages[b]	10.9	12.0	3.6	23.3	25.0	0.0
Tobacco	12.0	12.0	0.0	21.4	30.0	0.0
Cotton	0.0	0.0	100.0	8.2	12.0	0.0
Other agricultural products	0.0	0.0	0.0	10.3	15.0	1.6

a   Calculations of averages exclude four tariff lines that bear specific rates.
b   Calculations of averages only include non-alcoholic beverages and beer. Other alcoholic beverages bear a specific rate.

Source: WTO calculations, based on data provided by the Georgian authorities.

(3)   INDUSTRY

20.   Prior to independence, the Georgian economy was closely integrated with that of the Soviet Union; trade accounted for an estimated 40% of GDP, and nearly all exports were directed to, and three quarters of imports were from, the Soviet republics. The industrial sector accounted for about one third of the economy and although Georgia lacked cheap sources of energy, it produced energy-intensive products, such as steel pipes and locomotives, for export. The competitiveness of Georgia's heavy industry was dependent on the supply of natural gas from Turkmenistan at artificially low pieces, and on the inflated prices of its final products. The dissolution of the FSU had a serious effect on the Georgian economy: the prices of gas and oil rose dramatically in the early 1990s, making Georgia's heavy industry non-competitive and halting production in its industrial centres. Georgia's industrial sector currently accounts for around one fifth of GDP and comprises mining, manufacturing, energy, and construction.

(i)   Manufacturing

(a)   Main features

21.   The manufacturing sector experienced a sharp contraction in output during the initial phase of the transition, but aggressive privatization by State authorities has created a favourable environment for the restoration of industrial production. Under the Soviet central planning system, SOEs accounted for a large share of industrial production, such as energy production and distribution, water supply, oil refinery, ferrous metallurgical manufacturing, mining of manganese ore deposits, mechanical engineering, chemicals, and food processing. After independence, a number of these industries were no longer financially viable and had to shut down. After 2003, the new Government began a competitive privatization process, helping to attract domestic and foreign investors. During most of the review period, the performance of manufacturing industry, led by food, beverages and tobacco manufacturing, has shown double-digit growth. Growth in manufacturing has been driven

both by external demand for certain goods mainly for metals, cement, and fertilizers, and by increased domestic demand for processed foods, soft drinks, building materials, and timber.

22.   A 2009 World Bank study points out that there has been very limited investment in export-oriented agri-business and manufacturing.[6] It identifies a number of sectors that seem to offer the most potential for local and foreign investors: wine, fruit and vegetables; construction materials; apparel; and pharmaceuticals and medical devices.

(b)   Policies

23.   To enhance productivity growth and competitiveness, the Georgian authorities have pursued structural reforms on several fronts: privatization; enterprise, business regulatory, and institutional reforms; trade liberalization; the finance sector; infrastructure and utilities; standardization; and public-sector management. There is considerable evidence that the Government's economic reforms have created a favourable investment climate for the development of industry. Reforms in labour regulations and licensing have helped to facilitate Georgia's integration into international markets; in particular, a licensing and permit system, one of the most significant preconditions for ensuring the proper functioning of a liberal market economy. The authorities maintain that the Government has not prioritized any sectors with regard to industrial policy; its overall policy is to minimize state intervention in the market and to promote a business-friendly environment through economic and institutional reforms.

(ii)   Energy sector

24.   During the review period, Georgia, a net energy and fuel importer, has made good progress in energy sector reforms to address chronic power shortages and the poor financial state of electricity and gas companies. Reforms have addressed electricity sector debt, improvement in payment collection, better reporting of electricity services, and diversification of supply in the gas sector. Government implemented large tariff increases in 2006, helping to bring about a financially sustainable energy sector, while well-targeted electricity and gas subsidies helped protect the most vulnerable. Significant investment in the energy sector, both by the Government and private investors, including the rehabilitation of hydro and thermal power plants, electricity transmission lines and distribution networks, gas and electricity metering systems and better regulation of the entire sector, has made it more efficient and stable. The electricity and gas markets for industrial users were liberalized in 2006 and 2008 respectively. The Government has completed the privatization of assets in power generation and distribution.

(a)   Electricity

25.   According to the authorities, Georgia produced about 8.6 billion kilowatt-hours (kWh) of electricity in 2008 and consumed about 8.4 billion kWh. Currently, around 85% of Georgia's electricity demand is met from hydropower plants located in the western part of the country and the rest from thermal units located in the east. Increased hydropower capacity would better satisfy demand and also reduce Georgia's dependence on imported natural gas for power generation in winter.

26.   According to the World Bank, in 2003, the average electricity service was for only seven hours per day per household, and collections averaged 35%; by 2008 electricity was being provided almost 24 hours a day to paying customers and collections rose to 95%.[7] The reliability of

---

[6] World Bank (2009c).
[7] World Bank (2008).

electricity services has improved greatly due to investment in energy infrastructure and maintenance. Financial viability has strengthened with tariff reforms, implementation of consumer re-metering programmes, improved revenue collection, and reduction in the quasi-fiscal deficits in the sector. Privatization of power generation and distribution has improved management of operations. Generation is now mostly private, transmission is a mix of public and private, and distribution is private. With the completion of the 2007 privatization programme in power generation and distribution, the private sector has become the main operator, with the state shifting towards policy development and regulatory functions.

27.   A significant issue for Georgia's electricity sector is that despite improvements in supply, the system is overly dependent on one large hydropower plant, Enguri, located in a conflict zone: the dam is in Georgia and the turbines and generators in Abkhazia. The plant is jointly managed with a Russian company.[8]

(b)   Gas

28.   Unlike electricity, most of which is generated through hydroelectric power, gas is entirely imported. In 2007, 60% of this gas was imported from Russia and the remaining 40% from Azerbaijan. Supplies of natural gas from Azerbaijan have been increasing and in December 2008 an agreement was signed with Azerbaijan to supply Georgia with gas for five years using a pre-defined price scheme. The Georgian authorities maintain that Russian gas now represents an insignificant share in the national gas balance and the August 2008 armed conflict demonstrated the need for Georgia to build underground natural gas storage, which would reduce the risk of interruptions in supplies.

29.   In 2008, the gas market was completely deregulated, and all private companies have the right to purchase the volume of gas they require at the price they can negotiate with producers. According to the authorities, market deregulation should be viewed positively as it can foster competition between different importers.

(c)   Regulatory framework

30.   The Ministry of Energy is the main energy policy body. The main objectives of energy policy are: diversification of supply sources (to include harnessing the full potential of domestic hydropower resources); liberalization and deregulation of the market to attract competitive private investment; and the maximization of Georgia's benefits as an energy transit corridor. Moving towards more energy independence is critical given that energy imports, mainly oil and gas, have accounted for nearly one fifth of the total annual import bill during the review period, and are a significant contributory factor to the country's large trade deficit.

---

[8] The Georgian Government had to sign a memorandum of understanding with the Russian Inter RAO (the subsidiary of the state-owned electricity monopoly Inter RAO UES) in December 2008 on joint management of the power plant. According to the authorities, the final agreement has not yet been signed by the parties so the plant is managed only by Georgia. Russia's Inter RAO UES owns and operates the electricity distribution company that supplies electricity to the Georgian capital Tbilisi; overall, around 25% of electricity generation and 35% of distribution is controlled by that company. See Phillips (2008), p. 11.

31. The 1999 Laws on Electricity and Natural Gas[9] and on Oil and Gas constitute the basic legislative framework for the sector, which is overseen by the independent National Energy and Water Regulatory Commission. The Commission is responsible for regulating competition, dispute settlement, and issuing/withdrawing licences, as well for adopting rules and conditions related to electricity, gas, and water supply. Anti-monopoly regulations in the energy sector are provided in the 1999 laws. One of the main objectives is facilitation of competition, setting up transparent and equal mechanisms for economic agents, and elaboration of a tariff system to avoid monopolistic prices in energy and water supply.

(iii) Construction

32. Construction is one of the most dynamic sectors in the Georgian economy. In 2005 the sector grew by an estimated 14.1% (year-on-year), driven by the building of two hydrocarbons pipelines; the BTC oil pipeline became fully operational in mid-2006, and the gas pipeline followed in early 2007. Growth in construction slowed in 2006, but rebounded to 14.3% in 2007, as demand surged for private housing and development of the tourism sector in centres such as Batumi, on the Black Sea coast, and Tbilisi. The increase in building activity has had spillover effects into services such as telecommunications, and hotels and catering, with a consequent increase in employment and, with it, domestic demand. However, by 2008 there were signs that the boom in real estate had peaked, even before the military conflict with Russia.

33. The construction industry contributed around 7.8% of GDP and employed over 4% of the country's workforce in 2007. Between 2004 and 2007, growth was driven largely by expansion in the residential and commercial real estate market and infrastructure. According to the MoED, there are currently 88 real estate companies operating which are responsible for architectural design and for obtaining construction permits. Once a permit is obtained, the real estate company can begin to sell space in the planned residential/commercial building.

34. The 2005 Framework Law on licences and permits also applies to construction permits. It governs the regulatory framework of licences/permits and stipulates the rules and procedures for their issuance, amendment, and revocation. In addition, the Government adopted Resolution 140 on Construction Permit Issuance Procedure and Permit Times in August 2005. The resolution, amended several times, is part of an on-going effort to consolidate all construction regulations, starting from planning issues through to building commissioning. Resolution 57 on Construction Permit Issuance Procedure and Permit Times, a single legislative act, replaced Resolution 140 as of March 2009.

35. Since 2005, the Government has undertaken a comprehensive construction sector reform programme to simplify and streamline land-use regulations and the administrative procedures for issuing construction permits and occupancy certificates. This has doubtless been a factor in Georgia's rise from 152nd position in 2005 to 10th in 2009 in the "dealing-with-licenses" category of the World Bank Doing Business rankings. Changes in the construction industry regulatory framework significantly reduced the number of procedures required for obtaining a construction permit, on

---

[9] The Georgian Law on Electricity and Natural Gas established the legal base for regulating relations and activities of sole proprietors, physical persons, and legal entities in the areas of electricity system operation, wholesale electricity (capacity) trade, electricity generation, transmission, dispatch, distribution, import, export, and consumption, as well as in natural gas supply, import, export, transportation, distribution, and consumption, and promoting the functioning and development of the electricity and natural gas sectors in Georgia, based on market economy principles. The present law does not apply to exploration, production, processing and storage of natural gas, or to relations between the producer and supplier of natural gas or to electricity or natural gas transit through the territory of Georgia.

average from 29 to 12, while the average time required for obtaining permits was reduced from 285 days to 113 days.

(4)   SERVICES

36.   Services accounted for approximately 69% of Georgia's current GDP in 2008, up from 56% in 2002 and from an estimated 32% in 1998. Employment in the services sector remained more or less constant at around 37% of total employment during the period under review. Many of the services sold in Georgia are labour-intensive, low-tech services, and these are likely to fall in importance as the economy develops. Georgia has a small surplus on the balance of services within the current account, mainly reflecting income relating to oil and gas pipelines.

37.   The financial sub-sector has expanded rapidly, and telecommunications, real estate and rental, and restaurants and hotels have benefited from increasing FDI resources, helping them to realize above-average growth rates. High domestic demand contributed to growth of domestic trade services because most locally consumed products are imported. In this sense, both the wholesale and retail trades are to a considerable extent dependent on external trade transactions that have intensified through Georgia's highly liberalized tariff regime.

(i)   General Agreement on Trade in Services (GATS)

38.   In preparation for accession to the WTO, Georgia adopted new laws and amended existing legislation related to trade in services to make the legislative basis consistent with the WTO Agreements.[10] As part of its WTO accession process, Georgia offered mostly liberal access in the services sector with no discrimination against foreign suppliers across the modes of supply in a broad range of business services, financial services, telecommunication services, construction and related engineering services, professional services, tourism, and transport services. Georgia's Schedule of Specific Commitments on Services (GATS/SC/129) contains its legally binding market access commitments in respect of services. Notably, Georgia's commitments opened the way for foreign investors in virtually all sectors. Georgia took undertook commitments in 123 sub-sectors (out of 155) in 11 sectors. Under Georgia's WTO accession agreement energy-related services are largely liberalized. Georgia maintained restrictions in a few cases, especially in transportation, construction[11], and insurance but through reforms implemented during 2004-09, the authorities indicate that these have been liberalized. Georgia took MFN exemptions for measures in three sectors: transport services, fishing related services, and motion picture or video tape production services (GATS/EL/129).

39.   In the services negotiations in the Doha Round, Georgia's position is that it has unilaterally liberalized its services sector and therefore it has not made an initial offer.

---

[10] General laws related to services included the Constitution of Georgia; the Law on promotion and guarantees of investment activity; the Law on entrepreneurship; the Law on the legal conditions of foreigners; the Law on temporary entry, residence and exit of foreigners from Georgia; the Law on monopoly activities and competition; and the Bankruptcy Law of 25 July 1996.

[11] In the construction sector, not less than 50% of the entire staff of a service supplier of another member who wishes to establish a commercial presence in Georgia are required to be Georgian citizens. The Georgian insurance sector remains subject to some restrictions, mainly in relation to presence of natural persons, but these do not appear to be onerous.

(ii) Financial services

(a) Main features

40. In 2008, financial intermediation comprised 2.4% of GDP, up from 1.6% of GDP in 2003, as the banking sector expanded rapidly. The credit to GDP ratio increased from 8% in 2002 to 32% in 2008 and total assets of the banking system grew from 16% of GDP to over 46% of GDP. The number of individuals with bank accounts grew more than ten-fold, from an estimated 200,000 to over 2.2 million between 2003 and 2008. However, the financial sector is among the smallest relative to GDP in the Europe and Central Asia region, and remains dominated by banks. According to the Central Bank, nearly 99% of financial intermediation takes place through the banking system, meaning that the mobilization and transformation of financial resources into investment resources is carried out by banking institutions and not through the securities market, a situation that "is unlikely to change in the foreseeable future".[12] Apart from banking, the other sub-sectors comprise insurance, securities, microfinance institutions, and credit unions. According to the IMF, access to financial services and to credit is insufficient in particular in rural areas where banks are unlikely to open a branch unless they are sure of its profitability; this can make access to banks difficult.[13] The Georgian authorities indicate that four of the twelve regions in Georgia have less than one bank branch per 10,000 citizens.

(b) Banking sector

41. Georgia completed the privatization of its banking sector in 1995 and since then has maintained no restrictions on foreign ownership of banks. The NBG instituted bank consolidation and reform, imposing increasingly stringent reporting and capital requirements. Consequently, the number of banks fell sharply, from 247 in 1995 to 17 at the end of 2006, but rose to 21 in mid 2008, of which 16 are Georgian private banks. Although the banking sector has begun to consolidate in recent years, commercial banks remain risk-averse; most loans are still issued to finance trade and consumption, whereas access to loans for the industrial and agricultural sectors remains limited.

42. The financial sector is growing rapidly and there are no entry barriers to banks. Foreign investment, accounted for 36.4% of total bank capital in 2005, 61.7% in 2006, and 74.7% in 2009. Foreign participation in the banking system is significant with majority foreign ownership in ten banks, including private foreign investors, banks from the former Soviet Union, and international financial institutions and development agencies.[14] The six largest banks (Bank of Georgia, TBC Bank, Société Générale, Prokredit, VTB, HSBC) hold around 87% of the total assets of the sector, 90% of the total outstanding loans, and about 89% of deposits. Pressure for consolidation in the sector comes from the new minimum capital requirement regulation, which requires all banks to have

---

[12] National Bank of Georgia (2006), p. 5.

[13] IMF (2007), p. 3.

[14] In 2005 Russian, Kazakh, U.S., and German capital was invested in Georgian banks. In September 2006, the French bank Société Générale acquired 60% of one of the leading Georgian banks, Bank Republic. Société Générale holds about 11% of the market in terms of deposits and over 30% of the plastic cards in circulation in Georgia through its subsidiary. The Austrian Creditanstalt bought the EBRD's 11.8% stake in the Bank of Georgia, the second biggest bank, in 2006, on behalf of a range of institutional investors. The Russian Vneshtorgbank (VTB), the German Procredit, the Kazakh Turan Alem Bank and the Armenian Cascade Bank are also present, in addition to a number of multilateral funding organizations. There are branches of the Turkish Ziraat Bank and the Azeri Development Bank of the Caucasus in Tbilisi. According to the authorities, foreign investment has intensified with four new banks established with foreign capital since the beginning of 2007: the International Bank of Azerbaijan-Georgia (Azerbaijan), HSBC Bank Georgia (UK), Halyk Bank (Kazakhstan), and KOR Standard Bank (owned by the Dhabi Group based in the UAE).

paid-up capital of at least US$6.5 million by 2008. At the same time, the National Bank lists maintenance of competition in the banking sector as a priority in its Strategy for 2006-09.

43. Banks have been reluctant to lend to small farmers because small fragmented parcels of land are considered inadequate collateral. As a result, the small farm and small agri-business sectors remain under-served by the banking system and bank lending tends to be concentrated in trade and construction. The microfinance sub-sector comprises credit unions, non-government microfinance operators, and banks.

44. In the weeks after the August 2008 conflict, there was a temporary withdrawal of deposits but remedial measures, including the provision of liquidity, helped to return some deposits. Deposits and net loans at the end of June 2009 were considerably down compared with a year before, and while overall loan demand has remained low, banks have been unwilling to lend to other than their most reliable customers.

(c)   Bank performance

45. The banking system is generally sound but the interest rate spread remains relatively high due to a number of factors, including high operating costs, risks associated with collecting against collateral, and lack of good credit information (Table IV.5). Average spreads between lending (currently around 35%) and deposit rates have generally been declining but increased to 13.9% (in domestic currency) and remained at 9% (for foreign currency) in mid 2009.

Table IV.5
Performance indicators of commercial banks, 2004-09

	2004	2005	2006	2007	2008	2009 (June)
Capital adequacy ratio (%)	18.8	17.5	20.6	16.0	13.9	17.5
Non-performing loans (% of total loans)	6.2	3.8	2.5	2.6	12.7	18.7
Loans in foreign exchange (% of total loans)	86.7	76.2	73.8	68.6	73	77
Net open foreign exchange position[a]	7.4	7.5	3.7	5.0	1.7	8.8
Liquidity ratio (%)	45.0	33.3	41.5	37.2	28.3	31.4
Return on equity	10.0	14.9	15.3	9.6	-14.2	-4.14
Interest rate spread[b] (%)						
- in domestic currency	13.3	9.2	11.0	11.0	12.0	13.9
- in foreign currency	19.4	17.0	11.0	9.0	9	9.0

a   Percent of total regulatory capital.
b   Spread between reference lending and deposit rates.

Source: National Bank of Georgia.

46. Liquidity and solvency ratios have deteriorated but remain satisfactory overall, partly due to liquidity support from the NBG. According to the central bank, the decrease in the liquidity level can be explained by efforts of large banks to direct resources at their disposal to more profitable operations (loans), leading to a lower growth rate of liquid assets than of liabilities.[15] The authorities indicate that the FSA has decreased the prudential liquidity ratio from 30% to 20% as part of a set of counter-cyclical measures; however, banks continue to maintain high liquidity to safeguard against increased volatility of liabilities. Although bank soundness indicators are broadly adequate, the recent sharp increase in non-performing loans and the decline in profitability are concern. Asset quality risks seem to have been covered through adequate reserves for loan losses, and additional capital

---

[15] National Bank of Georgia (2008), p. 5.

injections from investors and parent groups allowed banks to increase the CAR to 17.6% in June 2009. The Georgian banking sector was moderately profitable during 2004/08, with a rate of return on equity (ROE) of between 10% and 14.2%; however, there has been a severe decline in profitability due to an increase in the expected loan loss reserve.

47.   There was rapid expansion of credit between 2004 and 2007 at an average annual rate of around 57%, possibly due partly to increased efficiency in the system, and to improvements in the (still unsatisfactory) legal environment, especially with respect to the recovery of bad loans.

(d)   Non-bank financial institutions

The insurance sector

48.   The insurance market is still quite small with 13 licensed insurance companies in Georgia. Private pension insurance is provided by seven private pension funds. Total written premiums collected in 2008 amounted to 1.46% of GDP; while this is small, the insurance market is growing dynamically, conditioned, according to the authorities, by the development of corporate health insurance products including life insurance.

49.   The process of aligning Georgian legislation in the insurance sector with international standards began in 1997. Up to 2008, the insurance sector was regulated by the 1997 Law on Insurance, amended in 1998 to abolish restrictions on foreign ownership of insurance companies, effective upon Georgia's accession to the WTO. Under the Ministry of Finance, supervision was carried out by the Insurance State Supervision Service of Georgia, an independent governmental body that coordinated insurance activity, secured the solvability of insurance companies, supervised insurance activity, and participated in the revision process for insurance policy and in its implementation. Since April 2008, the insurance sector is regulated by the FSA, which introduced a number of new rules, including increased solvency requirements for operators in the insurance market. The FSA is a member of the International Association of Insurance Supervisors (IAIS), and its main objectives are to establish a legal and regulatory environment that takes into account internationally recognized standards, and to facilitate the development of a solvent, fair, and competitive insurance market in Georgia.

Capital markets

50.   The Georgian stock exchange is tiny, and accounts for less than 1% of total financial intermediation in the country. About 157 companies are listed on the exchange but only a few stocks are regularly traded. The volume of trading was only US$24 million in 2007, and the capitalization of the market was around GEL 1.7 billion, 70% of which is due to one stock (the Bank of Georgia).[16] The Government is anxious to develop the exchange, and the Banking Strategy for the Period 2006-09 includes an ambitious programme of legislation, including electronic means of payment. But even on the most optimistic assumptions, the Georgian stock market will remain a minor element in the Georgian financial system for the foreseeable future.

51.   Until 2008, the primary legislation governing the securities market in Georgia was the Law on Securities Market adopted in December 1998 and amended in August 2003. Pursuant to the law, the National Securities Commission of Georgia (NSCG) was established in 1999 as an independent body in charge of supervising, licensing and regulating the securities market. As of 2008, the Financial Supervision Agency (FSA) took over these duties. In order to improve liquidity in the market, recent amendments to the securities law allowed the demutualization of the stock exchange and remote

---

[16] Nadibaidze (2008), p. 3.

trading in securities listed in so-called recognized stock exchanges without the need to establish a local presence.

(e)   Financial regulatory framework

52.   Prior to 2008, banks were required to hold a banking licence issued by the National Bank of Georgia (NBG). The National Bank based its administrative decisions on the 1995 Law on the national bank and the 1996 Law on commercial banks' activities. Foreign banks operated in accordance with Georgia's common banking legislation and were not subject to any special or additional requirements. A new law – the Global Competitiveness of the Financial Services Sector Act – was approved by Parliament in March 2008 to modernize the financial sector including: (i) establishing a single Financial Supervision Agency (FSA) for the banking and non-banking sectors (capital markets and insurance); (ii) strengthening the independence of the Central Bank, with first steps towards inflation targeting; (iii) demutualizing the stock exchange; and (iv) developing an international financial centre to attract foreign funding by offering tax exemptions to large international financial companies whose activity in Georgia does not exceed 10% of their financial turnover (Box IV.1).

53.   Amendments to the central bank law now make price stability the primary objective of the National Bank of Georgia (NBG), requiring it to target single-digit inflation by imposing a targeted inflation policy, in line with the authorities' commitment to keeping inflation to less than 10%. The NBG has been assigned the duty of the lender of last resort: if any commercial bank encounters financial difficulties that may lead to its bankruptcy and put the financial sector in jeopardy, the NBG is authorized to extend a loan of last resort to this bank in order to prevent a crisis. Usually, a loan of last resort is short term (up to three months), issued at a higher than market interest rate and is collateralized. However, under special circumstances the NBG may also extend longer-term and unsecured loans.

54.   The FSA was created as a fully independent agency with its own supervisory board, responsible for the consolidated supervision of banks, insurance companies, and securities firms, and for issuing licences to commercial banks and other participants of the financial sector, granting them the authority to conduct relevant business activities. Until 2008, three different entities regulated the financial sector in Georgia: in particular, the Supervision Department of the NBG was responsible for regulating activities of commercial banks, microfinance organizations, credit unions and foreign exchange bureaus; the National Securities Commission monitored the securities market; and the State Insurance Supervisory Service monitored the insurance companies. Pursuant to the 2007-08 amendments to the respective laws, the FSA was set up (merging the three entities) to regulate the financial sector.[17] The FSA of Georgia is an independent body; it is not subordinated to any other body or government official; it has a balance sheet and a seal of its own. The Agency is accountable to its Board and reports annually to Parliament. To carry out its activities, it receives funds from the NBG. Under Georgian law, the FSA has full authority to supervise the activities of commercial banks and other financial intermediaries. The aim of banking supervision, according to the Georgian authorities, is to balance safety and efficiency of the financial system (to avoid inappropriate or over-regulation) with being forward-looking in detecting and managing risks, thus protecting bank depositors' and other creditors' funds while upholding the principles of competition in the banking system.

---

[17] National Bank of Georgia online information. Viewed at: http://www.nbg.gov.ge/index.php?m=109.

Box IV.1: Global competitiveness of the Financial Services Sector Act 2008

The Act, adopted in March 2008, amends 17 laws regulating the financial services to enhance the stability and global competitiveness of the Georgian financial sector. The key changes include:

National Bank of Georgia, the Financial Services Authority (FSA) and streamlining of bank governance

The preservation of price stability is the main objective of the National Bank of Georgia. The NBG is required to declare annually its three-year rolling inflation (CPI) target, which cannot be higher than 10%. A band of 2% will be allowed for both over-shooting and under-shooting the target. In the event of either for four consecutive quarters, the NBG President will have to face a parliamentary vote of confidence.

The FSA was created under the auspices of the NBG to function autonomously as the sole regulator and supervisor of the financial services sector, including banking, securities, insurance and other areas. However, as of August 2009, draft legislation was being prepared for the merger of the FSA and the central bank to create a consolidated regulator/supervisor of the financial system.

To streamline the governance of commercial banks, executive directors will be allowed to serve on the supervisory board, creating a single-board governance regime. The banks are no longer be required to have an audit commission separate from the supervisory board.

Enhancement and streamlining of the anti-money laundering and "fit and proper" regulations

This includes improving the efficacy of the Financial Monitoring Service, the anti-money-laundering watchdog operating as a unit of the FSA, and increasing the transparency of the banking sector. The "fit and proper" criteria with regard to owners of significant (greater than 10%) stakes in Georgian banks are to be streamlined, with the burden of disclosure and compliance placed primarily on the bank shareholders, rather than on the banks themselves. The "see-through" procedures, enabling the regulator to assess and evaluate the identities of beneficial owners, will also be enhanced.

Taxation of financial instruments

Effective 1 January 2009, the act abolished tax on interest income received from deposits placed with licensed deposit-taking institutions and publicly-traded fixed income securities; capital gains on the securities admitted to trading on a local stock exchange with a free float exceeding 25%; and tax on dividend income from equities admitted to trading on a local stock exchange with a free float exceeding 25%.

International Financial Institutions (IFIs)

The status of IFI is to be introduced, enabling foreign and local investors to establish such institutions (in banking, insurance, reinsurance, securities, fund management and administration, custody, trust, and other areas) and avail themselves of the favourable tax regime. In addition, given that the IFIs are prohibited from deriving more than 10% of their revenues from domestic (Georgian) sources and from soliciting the business of local residents (except for high net worth individuals), they will be exempt from the local prudential regulations and supervision by the FSA (but will be subject to the local AML regulations). The concept of Experienced Investor Funds will be introduced, in order to establish Georgia as an attractive jurisdiction for fund administration and wealth management. Local stock exchanges will be allowed to quote securities in any currency (with the settlement taking place in Georgian lari). In order to attract qualified individuals to reside and establish business practice in Georgia, IFIs are required to employ a director who is a Georgian tax resident (but not citizen).

Stock exchange demutualization and other changes in the securities law

Changes are made in the securities law, allowing for the demutualization of local stock exchanges. Remote foreign membership of stock exchanges will be allowed, facilitating access to locally traded securities for broker-dealers licensed in any of the OECD countries without the need to establish a local subsidiary or be licensed and regulated by the FSA (provided they do not solicit business from local residents).

Source: WTO Secretariat, based on information provided by the Georgian authorities.

55.   Effective prudential regulation of the banking sector has contributed significantly to its rapid growth. For a decade or more, Georgia has maintained a simple bank licensing regime, under which there is only one type of bank licence, allowing licensed banks to engage in all banking activities and preventing excessive fragmentation of the sector. Georgian banks are allowed to pursue a universal banking model and the leading banks became involved through acquisitions in insurance, broker-dealer activities, wealth management, pensions, card processing, and related activities.

56.   Georgian banks are still primarily regulated on the basis of the Basle-1 rules of risk assessment. However, the regulatory framework is based on higher capital standards, which makes the Georgian banking system highly capitalized, allowing the FSA to decrease capital charges during a downturn as part of its counter-cyclical measures. The January 2004 Law on facilitating the elimination of legalisation of illegal incomes provides the basis for the work of the Financial Monitoring Service of the National Bank in countering money laundering. Société Générale, which is supervised by the National Bank of Georgia but also reports to the French Commission Bancaire, is regulated on the basis of Basle-II (as is HSBC), which is more self-regulatory than Basle-1 but better suited to the operations of highly sophisticated first-tier banks. According to the authorities, the FSA does not intend to fully adopt Basel-II any time soon, due to perceived inherent problems such as pro-cyclicality.

57.   The law on commercial bank activities was amended to improve the transparency of ownership and corporate governance of banks. In March 2006, the restriction under which one shareholder or a group of joint shareholders could hold no more than 25% of voting shares in a bank was abolished. A new law regulating the activity of microfinance organizations entered into force in August 2006. All joint-stock companies with more than 50 shareholders – currently about 1,800 companies in Georgia – are required to submit annual, semi-annual, and current reports prepared in accordance with internationally accepted accounting standards. Other developments in the Georgian banking sector include the creation of a credit information bureau in 2006, to help banks with risk assessment. Measures have also been taken to strengthen the process of bank audit. The Government originally proposed to introduce a deposit insurance scheme in 2007[18]; the idea was dropped but remains an element in the Banking Strategy for the Period 2006-09.

(iii)   Telecommunications

(a)   Main features

58.   All market segments including local, domestic long-distance, international long-distance, mobile, data, and internet are formally liberalized. However, there appears to be little competition, and fixed-line services are dominated by the incumbent operators. The fixed-line network has only limited coverage outside Tbilisi, and growth in the number of fixed-line telephone units stagnated between 2003 and 2007, although the total number of active fixed-line phone subscribers grew to about 618,000 in 2008 (Table IV.6). Fixed-line teledensity has barely reached 14.7%, with rural areas being particularly under-served. There are two major operators on the market: the privatized United Georgian Telecom and Akhali Kselebi. Those two companies, together with Akhtel Communications, control an estimated 90% of the market. United Georgian Telecom is the market leader, controlling 75% of local fixed-line networks, and serves 72% of local calls. It has 350,000 fixed-line subscribers,

---

[18] Georgia is one of the few countries without any state-sponsored bank deposit insurance arrangements due in part to the high dollarization of deposits, which reduces the credibility of state guarantees.

most of which are in Tbilisi. The company was privatized in 2006 when the Georgian-Kazakhstan company Black Sea Telecom Holding became the majority shareholder.[19]

Table IV.6
Electronic communications sector, 2001-08

	2001	2002	2003	2004	2005	2006	2007	2008
Revenues (GEL million)	261.4	331.8	454.1	588.9	703.7	1,001.4	1,113.6	1,312.63
Share of revenues in communications sector in GDP (%)	3.8	4.3	5.1	5.7	6.1	7.5	6.6	6.9
Revenue share by segment (%)								
Fixed telephony	..	..	37.4	35.3	35.1	29.8	29.5	29.0
Mobile telephony	..	..	58.3	60.2	60.3	64.9	63.2	63.3
Broadcasting	..	..	4.3	4.5	4.6	5.3	7.5	7.7
Subscribers of fixed communications networks ('000)	..	493.9	519.5	532.7	544.4	553.1	556.1	618
Mobile network subscribers ('000)	253	430	520	841	1,152	1,704	2,600	2,755
Total ISD end users	..	..	..	..	200,326	270,031	521,494	903,444

.. Not available.

Source: Georgian authorities.

59. The mobile telephone industry has been growing rapidly. In 2008, three mobile telephony operators provided services for over 2.7 million subscribers (with a penetration rate of about 60%) up from 430,000 subscribers (about 10% penetration rate) in 2002. Competition between these operators (Geocell, Magticom, and industel) has stimulated considerable growth in this market.[20]

60. The mobile market, dominated by Magticom and Geocell, is effectively a duopoly although the authorities state that there are no legislative or financial entry barriers for other companies to enter the market; Mobitel entered in 2007.

61. Internet use has also increased in recent years with the number of subscribers rising from about 26,000 in 2006 to over 107,000 by 2008. The dominant providers are Caucasus Online and United Telecom which, between them, have a market share of 85%.

(b)   Legislative framework

62. The communications sector in Georgia is currently regulated by the Georgian National Communications Commission (GNCC) and governed by the Law on Electronic Communications. The law was adopted in 2005 and, according to the authorities, is in compliance with all five European Union communications directives.[21] The GNCC is an independent sector-specific

---

[19] Two companies used to control the fixed infrastructure inherited from the state: Sakartvelos Electrosvyaz (Georgian United Telecommunications Company), and Sakartvelos Telekomi (Georgia Telecom). Both companies were fully privatized.

[20] Geocell, which is controlled by a Swedish-Finnish operator (TeliaSonera), and acquired a universal mobile telecommunications service (UMTS) licence in May 2006; MagtiCom, owned by a group of U.S. companies; and Mobitel, owned by VimpelCom (Russia), which launched mobile services in 2007. According to the most recent data available, Magticom led the market with approximately 1.2 million subscribers out of 1.7 illion in 2006 and covered about 97% of the populated area of Georgia. Magticom won public bids for new CDMA and 3G licences issued by GNCC in 2005.

[21] The law stipulates the basic principles for protection of the competitive environment in the sector: merger controls and abuses of dominant position (among others) are regulated. In regard to determination of dominant position, the legislation meets the requirements of international agreements (among them WTO

regulatory authority, established in 2000. Its main functions relate to licensing, spectrum monitoring, tariff setting in regulated areas, the administration of universal service, maintenance of a competitive environment, and other technical aspects connected to the communications sector. The Department for Information and Communication Technology in the Ministry of Economic Development is responsible for the development of sector policy.

63.   The mobile market has benefited from the regulatory approach to competition taken by the GNCC. The GNCC has recognized that there are two important factors in the development of a competitive mobile sector: interconnection fees and number portability. Interconnection charges are one of the biggest cost items for new entrants and could constitute a significant barrier to development of potential competition as existing operators have an incentive to raise the cost of making/receiving calls to new networks, thus making it unattractive for consumers to switch to newer operators in the market. Interconnection charges are regulated by the GNCC (and were decreased by 21% in 2008), which also set a cap on the interconnection fee charged; it has also facilitated mobile number portability, permitting consumers to switch operator while keeping their cell number.[22]

(iv)   Transit and transport

64.   For centuries, Georgia has been a trading route linking Europe to Asia. In recent years, it has emerged as a strategic transit corridor for pipelines carrying Caspian oil and natural gas to world markets. Georgia plays an important role in the existing and planned projects for the transportation of oil and natural gas along the South Caucasus transit system outside the territory of the Russian Federation and Iran. While this yields a certain amount of revenue in transit fees, its main importance for Georgia is in helping it to establish itself as a guarantor of western energy security.

(a)   Transit

Oil and gas pipelines

65.   The Baku-Tbilisi-Ceyhan (BTC) oil pipeline has a current throughput capacity of 1 million barrels of per day (bpd) – around 1% of the world's daily production – of crude from BP's Azerbaijan offshore Azeri oilfields to export terminals at the Turkish port of Ceyhan in the Mediterranean. It is capable of carrying 1.2 million bpd with small upgrades, and 1.6 million bpd with additional pumping stations. The pipeline extends 1,750 km across all three countries, of which 249 km is in Georgia. The macroeconomic impact of the BTC pipeline, commissioned in September 2005, is reflected in: the sectoral contribution to GDP growth with the expansion of the construction sector and related services sector activity; the fiscal accounts, as higher non-tax revenues; and the balance of payments, initially in the construction phase as large pipeline-related FDI inflows, and after pipeline commissioning, as higher exports of services.

66.   The Baku-Supsa oil pipeline, opened in 1999, has an initial throughput capacity of 150,000 bpd of Azeri oil and is capably of carrying larger volumes with additional pumping stations. The pipeline constructed in the late 1990s and operated by British Petroleum, runs 814 km from Baku to the Georgian port of Supsa. Georgia also serves as a transit corridor for Kazakh oil (produced by the Chevron-led TCO consortium at Tengiz; crude oil is transported by barge across the Caspian Sea to Dupendi (near Baku), and is then moved by railcars.

General Agreement on Trade in Services). The law prohibits the use of subsidies in the provision of communications service.

[22] GNCC resolutions No. 189/9-2008 regulates interconnection charges for both the mobile and fixed-line network. Number portability will be facilitated by a new numbering plan to be elaborated by 2010.

67.   The Baku-Tbilisi-Erzerum natural gas pipeline, another BP-led Caspian development in the same corridor of land as the BTC pipeline, links the Shah Deniz gas and gas-condensate field in Azerbaijan to Erzerum in Turkey.   At full capacity, the 692 km pipeline will export up to 20 billion cubic meters of gas a year. Currently it is operating at a capacity of 8 billion cubic meters but is scheduled to increase production to supply natural gas via Turkey to Greece and Italy and onward through the Nabucco pipeline to Eastern and central Europe.

68.   For Azerbaijan, Georgia is a very significant export outlet and even after the events of August 2008, nearly all of the Azeri exports of oil and gas was via Georgian territory. Tariffs paid by oil and gas shippers for Georgian transit are not substantial. The BTC oil pipeline is expected to provide Georgia with transit fees of up to US$40 million per annum by 2009, while the SCP gas pipeline will provide an additional US$11 million in tariff payments. In order for Georgia to fully benefit from the BTC and SCP pipelines, transparency in revenue management will be essential. Gas received as a transit fee at full capacity of the SCP gas pipeline operation will be enough to meet half of Georgia's current demand. Georgia has the right to purchase another 5% under the terms of the concession agreement.

Georgian ports

69.   Poti and Batumi, Georgia's two major Black Sea ports, play a major role in the transit corridor system and in regional economic development. Poti, the main port facility for the entire region, handled 8 million tonnes in general liquid and dry cargoes in 2008, and 210,000 containers (Table IV.7). Poti terminal can handle 45,000 tankers and has a capacity for 60,000 bpd. The port is being refurbished to develop new terminals and increase freight capacity; on an annual basis, the sea port can handle 6.7 million tonnes of dry cargo and 3 million tonnes of liquid cargo. The port suffered limited damage from Russian bombing in the August 2008 armed conflict but has endured revenue losses in consequence.

Table IV.7
Transported cargo by mode, 2006-08
(Million tonnes)

Transport mode	Transit			Import			Export			Total		
	2006	2007	2008	2006	2007	2008	2006	2007	2008	2006	2007	2008
Railway	16.2	14.4	13.8	2.7	3.6	3.5	1.2	1.4	1.5	20.1	19.4	18.8
Road	0.8	1.1	1.4	0.9	1.1	1.2	0.3	0.2	0.2	2.0	2.4	2.8
Civil aviation ('000)	0	0	0	6.9	9.7	14.6	1.2	2.4	2.5	8.1	12.1	17.1
Total	17	15.5	15.2	3.6	4.7	4.7	1.5	1.6	1.7	22.1	21.8	21.6
Sea ports												
Poti	3.7	4.2	4.5	1.7	2.3	2.4	1.2	1.2	1.1	6.6	7.7	8.0
Batumi	12.4	10.2	7.8	0.4	0.4	0.3	0.3	0.6	0.5	13.1	11.2	8.6
Supsa	5.6	0	0.6	0	0	0	0	0	0	5.6	0	0.6
Kulevi	0	0	1.3	0	0	0	0	0	0	0	0	1.3
Total	21.7	14.4	14.2	2.1	2.7	2.7	1.5	1.8	1.6	25.3	18.9	18.5

Source: Georgian authorities.

70.   The port of Batumi is one of the deepest water ports in the Black sea. Both an oil terminal and seaport, it has a handling capacity of 15 million tonnes of oil and 2.5 million tonnes of dry cargo per year. The port shipped 11.2 million tonnes in 2007, of which 9.6 million tonnes were oil and oil products; tonnage declined to 8.6 million tonnes in 2008, of which 7.2 million tonnes were oil and oil and oil products. The port belongs to Kazakhstan's state-owned oil company KazMunaiGas.

71.   The new oil terminal of Kulevi is located to the north of Poti port. It is owned by Azerbaijan's state-owned company SOCAR. With a capacity of 4 million tonnes of liquid cargo per year, it handled 1.3 million tonnes in 2008.

Railways and roads

72.   Georgia's rail system accounted for 87% of the volume of non-machine cargo in 2008. Railways transported nearly 19 million tonnes of freight in 2008: 73% consisted of transit traffic[23], primarily oil and gas products; 19% import traffic; and only 8% export traffic. The Georgian railroad system is vital for Armenia's transportation, providing essential access to Georgian ports, and the rail transit infrastructure in the South Caucasus, connecting the port of Baku to the Georgian ports, has become a vital export line for Azerbaijan, Turkmenistan, and Kazakhstan, starting with oil and oil products and expanding into substantial freight volumes of grains, minerals, and fertilizers.

73.   Georgia's non-oil transit potential remains largely untapped; Georgia accounts for a relatively small share of the non-oil trade of the Central Asian republics and that of the two other South Caucasus countries, Armenia and Azerbaijan. Factors that contribute to underperformance include poor road conditions and long transit times. Road infrastructure improvement is one of the stated priorities in the BDD, the Government's main policy document, and various projects are under way in conjunction with several institutions, including the World Bank, the Japanese International Cooperation Agency, the Asian Development Bank, and the Millenium Challenge Corporation. Construction, rehabilitation, and maintenance works on Georgian roads are managed by the Road Department in the Ministry of Regional Development and Infrastructure.

(b)   Regulatory framework for the transport sector

74.   The Georgian National Commission for Transport Regulation regulated the sector until 2007, when the Unified Transport Administration (UTA), under the Ministry of Economic Development, assumed responsibility for the technical regulation of the road and maritime transport, and civil aviation. The UTA develops and endorses technical regulations on safety and security, and issues licences for transport operators. In a further recent change, the Ministry of Regional Development and Infrastructure became the overall regulatory authority.

75.   The main transport-related legislation comprises the Rail Code; the Civil Aviation Code; the Maritime Code; and the Law on Road Transport with their subordinate rules and technical regulations. According to the authorities, the basic thrust of government policy is ensuring safety and security, improving infrastructure, achieving the maximum feasible liberalization, maximizing Georgian transit potential, and improving regional cooperation and cooperation with international organizations.

76.   The rehabilitation of decaying physical infrastructure is important to enable the country to take advantage of its geographic position as an important transit link between the South Caucasus, Central Asia, and Europe. The railways are still operated as an unbundled state-owned company although some restructuring efforts have been made. The authorities stress that it is a profitable company able to invest in its infrastructure. Georgian Railways was granted the right to manage its cargo policy independently. Simplified tariff rates were introduced in 2007 with a view to attract additional cargo flows.

77.   When the Civil Aviation Authority was closed down in 2006, its functions were transferred to the National Commission and subsequently to the Unified Transport Administration. There is a need

---

[23] For a fuller analysis, see Lashkhi et al. (2008), p. 25.

to strengthen regulatory, and in particular safety, oversight in order to improve the safety performance of Georgian carriers. Georgia actively pursues a policy of liberalization of air traffic in order to promote competition. In 2005, Georgia announced an open skies policy with a view to abolishing restrictions on the number of authorized air carriers, and on capacity, frequency, and destinations. Georgia has proposed to change the law on licensing aviation activities, to open investment in Georgian carriers to foreigners. Georgia has also started negotiations with the European Commission on a comprehensive aviation agreement. The Batumi International Airport has been modernized, and the new Tbilisi International Airport was officially opened in February 2007. The Government states that the civil aviation authority cooperates actively with the International Civil Aviation Organization (ICAO) and other organizations on safety and security.

(v)   Tourism

78.   During the Soviet period, mass tourism was a major industry for Georgia, with around 5 million visitors a year mostly from various parts of the FSU. Tourist numbers are now only a fraction of what they were, but expanded more than three-fold between 2000 and 2008, from 387,000 to nearly 1.3 million (Table IV.8). Georgia, more than ever, is mainly visited by its immediate neighbours with Armenia, Azerbaijan, and Turkey accounting for over three-quarters of tourist arrivals. Figures made available by the authorities for the first seven months of 2009 indicate a small increase (0.3%) in the number of visitors compared with the same period in 2008 with the increase mainly accounted for by Azerbaijan. The authorities state that average expenditure per tourist is around US$815 and the average length of stay is 10.5 days. Tourists arrive mainly by air transport.

Table IV.8
International tourist arrivals and estimate share of GDP, 2000 and 2004-09

	2000	2004	2005	2006	2007	2008	2009[a]
Total ('000)	387	368	560	983	1,052	1,290	750
Share by source (%)							
CIS	57.4	59.5	65.3	64.5	62.4	60.8	61.9
Turkey	21.7	20.3	19.6	19.5	23.6	27.2	26.9
USA	2.3	2.6	2.3	1.7	1.4	1.2	1.1
Other	18.6	17.6	12.8	14.3	12.6	10.8	10.1
Estimated share of GDP of tourism related revenues (%)	3.2	4.1	4.5	4.0	4.1	3.7	..

..   Not available.

a   Seven months (Jan-July).

Source: WTO calculations, based on data from the Department of Tourism and Resorts of Georgia. Viewed at: http://www.dotr.gov.ge/eng/statistics.php; GDP shares provided by Georgia authorities.

79.   According to the authorities, the share of tourism revenues in Georgia's GDP has hovered around 4% since 2004. Tourism-related investments have seen impressive growth in recent years, reaching over US$1 billion by 2008. In terms of policies to encourage and develop tourism, procedures for issuing visas have been simplified. There is no visa requirement for nationals of Israel, Japan, Canada, USA and EU countries, nor for CIS nationals, except citizens of the Russian Federation and Turkmenistan. Visitors able to enter Georgia without a visa are allowed to stay for 90 days, and passengers on cruise ships who stay in Georgia for less than 72 hours do not require visas. According to the Tax Code, since 2006, tour operators' incoming tourist revenue has been exempted from VAT.

80.   Regarding basic infrastructure development, the authorities maintain that roads and highways, and energy and water supply systems are developing rapidly, with positive results for the tourism business. Tbilisi and Batumi are serviced by new modern airports approved for full membership in the European Civil Aviation Conference, with direct flights to 32 cities. Currently two Marriott hotels and one Sheraton hotel provide upmarket accommodation in Tbilisi, while the SAS Radisson hotel, Hyatt, Kempinski, and Intercontinental are under construction and Accor and Hilton hotels are scheduled for construction.

81.   To assist with developing the country's competitive advantage in tourism, the Government signed an agreement with the U.S. Trade and Development Agency in 2007 for the America-Georgia Business Council and others to develop a National Tourism Development and Investment Plan and Strategy. Together with the Georgia Department of Tourism and Resorts, a review of tourism policies, institutions, and infrastructure found substantial tourism potential but also serious impediments in terms of room stock, access to sights and attractions, and infrastructure.

REFERENCES

Asian Development Bank (2007), *Country Economic Report: Georgia.* Viewed at: http://www.adb.org/ Documents/CERs/GEO/CER-GEO-2007.pdf.

CASE, *Economic Feasibility, General Economic and Implications of a Free Trade Agreement between the European Union and Georgia,* Network Reports, No. 79 (2008), Warsaw. Viewed at: www.case-research.eu/upload/publikacja_plik/20963402_rc70.pdf.

EC Commission (2008), *Eastern Partnership, S*taff working document. Viewed at: http://ec.europa. eu/external_relations/eastern/docs/sec08_2974_en.pdf.

EC Commission (2009), *Implementation of the European Neighbourhood Policy in 2008: Progress Report on Georgia.* Viewed at: http://ec.europa.eu/world/enp/pdf/progress2009/sec09_513_en.pdf.

European Parliament (2008), *Analysis of the EU's Assistance to Georgia,* EP Briefing Paper, August. Viewed at: http://www.europarl.europa.eu/activities/committees/studies/download.do?file=22871).

Georgian Law Review (2005), GEPLAC Activities: *Analysis of the Draft Customs Code,* Vol. 8, No. 3-4. Viewed at: http://www.geplac.org/newfiles/reports/Draft%20Customs%20Code,%20 Avizienis.pdf.

Georgian Law Review (2006), *GEPLAC Activities: The New Competition Policy in Georgia.* Vol. 9, No. 1-2. Viewed at: http://www.geplac.org/files/50258_141_483576_The_%20New_Competition _Policy.pdf.

Government of Georgia (2007), *Basic Data and Directions for 2008-2011*, Tbilisi. Viewed at: http://www.imf.ge/aattach/285.pdf.

Gylfason, T. and E. Hochreiter (2008), *Growing Apart? A Tale of Two Republics: Estonia and Georgia,* IMF Working Paper, WP/08/235. Viewed at: http://www.imf.org/ external/pubs/ft/wp/2008/ wp08235.pdf.

Heritage Foundation (2009), *The 2009 Index of Economic Freedom.* Viewed at: http://www.heritage.org/index/ Country/Georgia.

IMF (2007), *Financial Sector Assessment Georgia.*

IMF (2009a), *Georgia: 2009 Article IV Consultation and Second Review under the Stand-By Arrangement*, Staff Report No. 09/127. Viewed at: http://www.imf.org/external/pubs/ft/2009/cr09 127.pdf.

IMF (2009b), *Georgia: Letter o f Intent.* Viewed at: http://www.imf.org/external/np/loi/2009/geo/ 073009.pdf.

IMF (2009c), *Georgia: Third Review under the Stand-By Arrangement,* IMF Country Report No. 09/267, August. Viewed at: http://www.imf.org/external/pubs/ft/scr/2009/cr09267.pdf.

Independent International Fact-Finding Mission on the Conflict in Georgia (2009), Report, September. Viewed at: http://www.ceiig.ch/Report.html.

International Finance Corporation (2008), *Georgia: After Three Years of Licensing Reform – Analytical Note.* Viewed at: http://www.ifc.org/ifcext/georgiasme.nsf/Attachments ByTitle/LicensingPolicy PaperEng/$FILE/ LicensingPolicyPaper.pdf.

Ivianiashvili-Orbeliani, G. (2009), "Globalization and National Competitiveness of Georgia", *Caucasian Review of International Affairs,* Vol. 3. Viewed at: http://cria-online.org/Journal/6/Done_ Globalization%20and %20National%20Competitiveness%20 of%20georgia_Orbeliane.pdf.

Lashkhi, I. et al. (2008), *Georgian Railway Problems and Perspectives,* Paper of the Open Society Georgia Foundation, Tbilisi. Viewed at: http://www.osgf.ge/data/file_db/ News/RAILWAY%20 Final%20ENG _9saox0TNn1.pdf.

Nadibaidze, L. (2008), *Waiting for a push: A quick overview Georgia's capital markets.* Viewed at: http://www.nbg.gov.ge/uploads/discussion/dp_nadibaidze_20.09.2008.pdf.

National Bank of Georgia (2006), *Georgian Banking System Development Strategy for 2006-2009.* Viewed at: http://www.nbg.gov.ge/uploads/publications/thematicpublications/nbg7.9nbg strategyeng.pdf.

National Bank of Georgia (2008), *Financial Stability Report 2008.* Viewed at: http://www.nbg.gov.ge/uploads/publications/finstability/nbg7.4financiaostabilityreport2008eng.pdf.

OECD (2009), *Competition Policy and the Informal Economy – Note by the Secretariat*, in document DAF/COMP/GF(2009)2. Viewed at: http://www.oecd.org/dataoecd/23/25/42062211.pdf.

Office of the State Minister of Georgia for European and Euro-Atlantic Integration (2009), *Georgia's Progress Report on Implementation of the ENP Action Plan in 2008.* Viewed at: http://www.amcham.ge/res/Bullets_on_+stPage/ENP/Progress_report_ENP_APImplem.pdf.

Phillips, D. (2008), *Post-Conflict Georgia, Policy Paper of the Atlantic Council of the United States.* Viewed at: http://www.acus.org/files/publication_pdfs/65/Post-Conflict%20Georgia.pdf.

Schneider, F. and D. Enste (2002), *The Shadow Economy: An International Survey,* Cambridge University Press, Cambridge.

Transparency International Georgia (2003), *Corruption Perception Index.* Viewed at: http://www.transparency.org/policy_research/surveys_indices/epi/2003.

Transparency International Georgia (2008a), *Competition in Georgia.* Viewed at: http://www.transparency.ge/files/215_476_979453_TI%20GEORGIA%20Competition%20in%20Ge orgia%20[ENG].pdf.

Transparency International Georgia (2008b), *Corruption Perception Index.* Viewed at: http://www.transparency.org/policy_research/surveys_indices/epi/2008.

Transparency International Georgia (2008c), *Food Safety in Georgia.* Viewed at: http://www.transparency.ge/ files/215_509_501247_FOOD%20SAFETY%20ENG.pdf.

UN and World Bank (2009), *Georgia: Joint Needs Assessment Progress Report,* 30 June.

UNDP (2008), *Georgia Human Development Report: the Reforms and Beyond,* Tbilisi, Georgia. Viewed at: http://undp.org.ge/new/files/24_278926712_nhdr2008-final-eng.pdf.

U.S. Department of State (2008), *Georgia: 2008 Investment Climate Statement.* Viewed at: http://www.state.gov/e/eeb/ifd/ 2008/10087.htm.

World Bank (2008), *International Development Association and International Finance Corporation: Country Partnership Strategy Progress Report for Georgia for the period FY06-FY09.* Viewed at: http://www-wds.worldbank.org/external/default/WDSContentServer/WDSP/IB/2008/05/13/0003349 55_200805 13061107/ Rendered/PDF/433540CASP0P101300and0IFCR200810123.pdf.

World Bank (2009a), *Doing Business 2010 Georgia.* Viewed at: http://www.doingbusiness.org/ Documents/CountryProfiles/GEO.pdf.

World Bank (2009b), *Georgia Poverty Assessment.* Viewed at: http://www-wds.worldbank.org/ external/default/WDSContentServer/WDSP/IB/2009/04/29/000350881_20090429111740/Rendered/P DF/444000ESW0P1071C0Disclosed041281091.pdf.

World Bank (2009c), *Georgia Manufacturing Sector Competitiveness Assessment.* Investment Climate Advisory Services (ICAAS). Viewed at: http://www.ifc.org/ifcext/georgiasme.nsf/ AttachmentsByTitle/2GeorgiaManufacturingSectorCompetitivenessAssessmentExe SumEng/$FILE/2 GeorgiaManufacturingSectorCompetitivenessAssessmentExeSumEng.pdf.

World Bank-European Commission (2008), *Georgia Public Expenditure and Financial Accountability,* Public Financial Management Assessment, Report No. 42886-GE, November. Viewed at: http://www-wds.worldbank.org/external/default/WDSContentServer/WDSP/IB/2009/ 01/29/00033303 8_20090129230214/Rendered/PDF/428860ESW0GE0P1010disclosed0Jan0281.pdf.

World Economic Forum (2008), *Global Competitiveness Report 2008-2009.* Viewed at: http://www.esmap.org/filez/pubs/PnP16633.pdf.

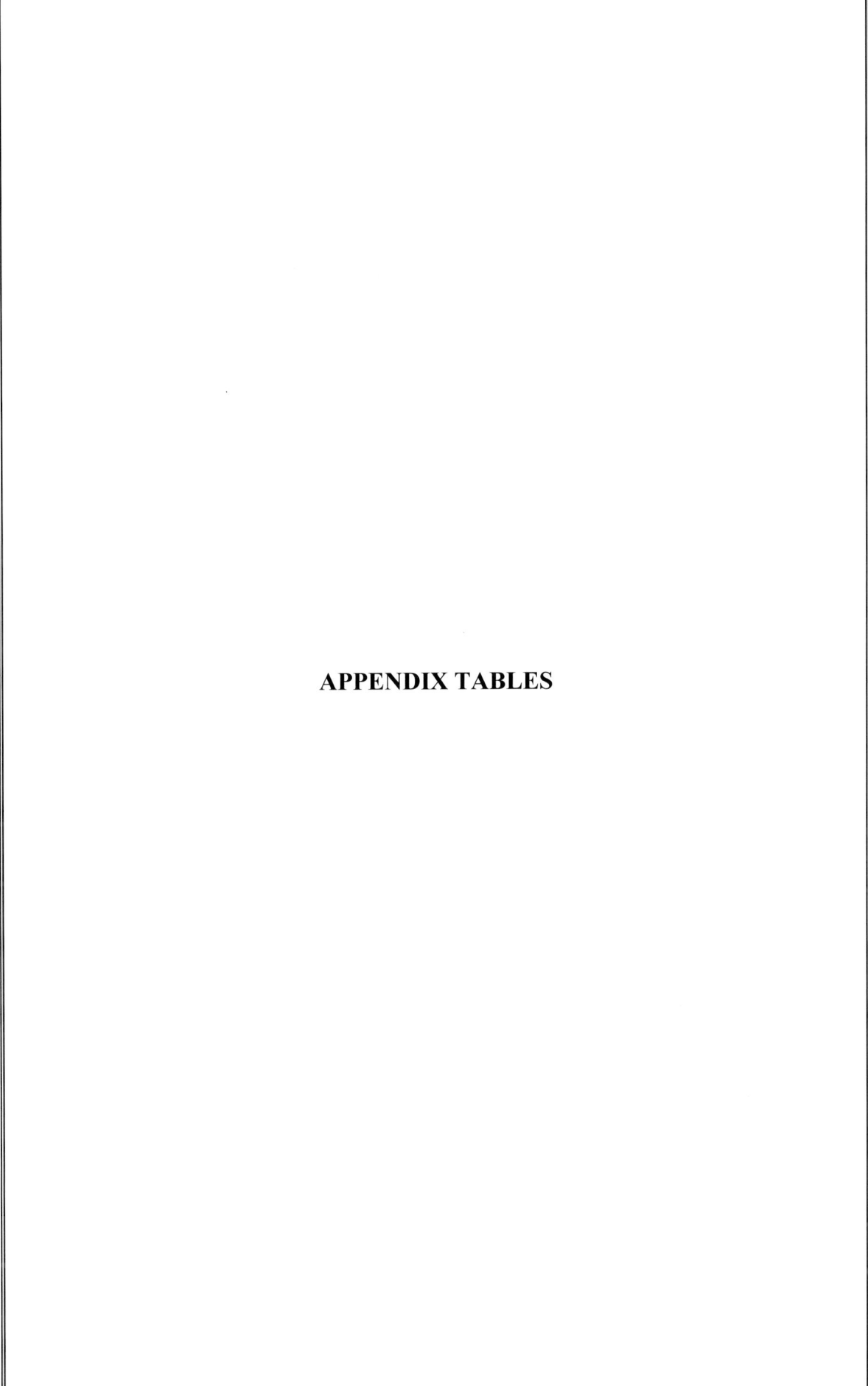

APPENDIX TABLES

Table AI.1
Merchandise exports by product group, 2002-08
(US$ million and per cent)

	2002	2003	2004	2005	2006	2007	2008
Total exports (US$ million)	346.3	465.3	648.8	866.2	991.5	1,232.9	1,497.5
				(Per cent of total)			
Total primary products	58.5	67.6	60.8	57.3	49.1	49.5	41.5
Agriculture	32.0	37.7	33.2	37.0	25.7	26.3	18.3
Food	29.7	34.9	31.0	34.9	23.5	24.0	16.5
1124 Spirits	1.6	2.8	2.9	3.4	3.0	4.7	3.9
1121 Wine of fresh grapes (including fortified wine)	9.6	9.2	7.5	9.4	4.2	2.5	2.7
1110 Non-alcoholic beverage, n.e.s.	5.8	6.8	5.1	6.1	4.7	4.4	2.6
0577 Edible nuts fresh, dried	2.0	2.7	2.7	8.1	5.7	5.3	2.1
Agricultural raw material	2.2	2.8	2.2	2.1	2.1	2.3	1.8
2484 Wood of non-coniferous, sawn of a thickness > 6 mm	1.4	1.9	1.4	1.2	1.1	1.2	1.0
Mining	26.5	29.9	27.6	20.3	23.4	23.2	23.2
Ores and other minerals	19.2	24.4	23.9	17.0	20.2	19.0	20.0
2831 Copper ores and concentrates	3.8	5.0	4.9	4.2	8.0	6.4	7.9
2823 Other ferrous waste and scrap	8.8	11.0	12.7	8.5	5.5	5.2	6.4
2882 Other non-ferrous base metal waste and scrap, n.e.s.	2.9	4.5	2.9	2.7	4.5	4.5	3.1
2822 Waste and scrap of alloy steel	1.8	1.9	2.1	1.2	1.8	2.6	2.1
Non-ferrous metals	1.9	0.4	0.2	0.1	0.3	0.5	0.2
Fuels	5.5	5.0	3.5	3.2	3.0	3.7	3.0
3330 Crude oils of petroleum and bituminous minerals	1.9	2.6	1.5	2.7	2.6	2.3	1.6
3510 Electric energy	1.9	1.0	0.0	0.4	0.2	1.4	1.1
Manufactures	33.2	28.0	36.2	38.7	46.0	44.9	51.7
Iron and steel	4.9	6.4	7.7	9.8	9.4	13.4	19.5
6715 Other ferro-alloys (excl. radio-active ferro-alloys)	3.6	4.1	5.4	7.8	8.5	12.2	15.6
6714 Ferro-manganese	0.9	1.5	1.2	1.5	0.5	0.8	2.2
Chemicals	7.0	6.2	6.8	6.7	7.9	9.6	10.5
5621 Mineral or chemical fertilizers, nitrogenous	3.5	4.0	4.4	4.1	4.7	4.6	7.0
5429 Medicaments, n.e.s.	0.8	0.6	0.4	0.4	0.8	1.2	1.3
Other semi-manufactures	0.5	0.8	1.8	2.8	4.3	7.2	6.3
6612 Portland cement and similar hydraulic cements	0.0	0.0	0.7	2.0	2.9	5.2	5.3
Machinery and transport equipment	19.2	13.1	18.7	17.0	20.8	12.4	12.9
Power generating machines	0.4	0.6	0.6	0.3	0.8	0.5	0.2
Other non-electrical machinery	1.7	1.4	2.1	3.4	5.6	2.2	1.1
Agricultural machinery and tractors	0.0	0.1	0.1	0.1	0.2	0.0	0.0
Office machines & telecommunication equipment	0.5	0.4	0.2	0.1	0.2	0.3	0.3
Other electrical machines	0.3	0.3	0.2	0.2	0.2	0.6	0.4
Automotive products	0.5	0.7	1.1	2.8	7.1	6.1	7.9
7812 Motor vehicles for the transport of persons, n.e.s.	0.2	0.2	0.6	2.1	5.1	5.7	7.6
Other transport equipment	16.0	9.8	14.5	10.3	6.9	2.7	3.0
7911 Rail locomotives, external powered	0.4	0.4	0.3	0.1	0.1	0.5	2.1
Textiles	0.1	0.1	0.1	0.0	0.0	0.0	0.1
Clothing	0.4	0.7	0.3	1.0	1.2	1.2	1.3
Other consumer goods	1.1	0.8	0.9	1.3	2.4	0.9	1.0
Other	8.3	4.4	2.9	4.0	4.9	5.6	6.9
9710 Gold, non-monetary (excl. gold ores and concentrates)	8.3	4.4	2.9	4.0	4.9	5.6	6.7

Source: UNSD Comtrade database, SITC Rev.3.

Table AI.2

Merchandise imports by product group, 2002-08

(US$ million and per cent)

	2002	2003	2004	2005	2006	2007	2008
Total imports (US$ million)	793.3	1,140.9	1,847.0	2,490.9	3,674.5	5,214.1	6,055.7
				(Per cent of total)			
Total primary products	43.1	37.2	39.3	38.3	37.0	34.9	35.9
Agriculture	21.4	18.5	21.4	17.8	16.9	16.3	15.9
Food	20.5	18.1	20.9	17.4	16.4	15.7	15.3
0412 Other wheat (including spelt) and meslin, unmilled	1.9	1.1	2.9	1.4	2.4	2.5	1.6
0461 Flour of wheat or of meslin	1.1	0.9	2.6	1.8	0.8	0.9	1.2
1222 Cigarettes containing tobacco	2.4	1.8	1.5	0.6	0.6	0.7	1.0
4215 Sunflower seed or safflower oil, and their fractions	0.4	0.3	0.9	0.9	0.6	0.6	0.8
0123 Poultry, meat and offal	1.4	0.9	0.5	0.6	0.6	0.7	0.7
0989 Food preparations, n.e.s.	0.6	0.3	0.3	0.4	0.4	0.5	0.7
Agricultural raw material	0.9	0.4	0.5	0.4	0.5	0.6	0.5
Mining	21.7	18.7	17.9	20.5	20.1	18.7	20.0
Ores and other minerals	0.5	0.4	0.4	0.3	0.4	0.7	1.5
2877 Manganese ores and concentrates	0.0	0.0	0.1	0.0	0.0	0.4	1.2
Non-ferrous metals	0.3	0.2	0.3	0.2	0.3	0.4	0.4
Fuels	20.8	18.0	17.3	19.9	19.4	17.6	18.0
3432 Natural gas, in the gaseous state	6.1	5.3	4.0	3.5	5.6	5.5	3.3
Manufactures	56.6	62.4	58.9	60.1	60.9	59.8	63.6
Iron and steel	2.6	10.9	6.6	2.5	2.9	4.4	4.8
Chemicals	13.4	11.6	9.9	9.6	9.0	8.5	9.1
5429 Medicaments, n.e.s.	7.0	5.2	3.9	3.4	2.7	2.4	2.6
Other semi-manufactures	7.2	6.9	7.4	8.7	8.6	8.5	9.5
6612 Portland cement and similar hydraulic cements	0.1	0.2	0.3	0.5	0.5	0.6	0.9
6624 Non-refractory brick, tiles, pipes, etc.	0.4	0.3	0.5	0.5	0.6	0.5	0.7
Machinery and transport equipment	25.4	25.6	26.7	29.4	28.9	27.8	29.2
Power generating machines	0.6	2.9	2.8	3.0	0.8	0.4	0.4
Other non-electrical machinery	7.9	7.3	7.1	5.5	6.3	6.4	6.2
Agricultural machinery and tractors	0.4	0.3	0.1	0.2	0.5	0.4	0.2
Office machines & telecommunication equipment	5.7	4.2	4.0	4.5	6.3	6.2	6.8
7643 Radio or television transmission apparatus	2.1	1.3	0.8	1.0	1.5	1.9	2.3
7611 Color television receivers	0.2	0.2	0.5	0.6	0.7	0.7	0.7
7641 Electrical apparatus for line telephony/telegraphy	0.6	0.8	0.2	0.2	0.4	0.4	0.6
Other electrical machines	2.9	2.8	3.3	3.7	3.6	4.0	4.4
7731 Insulated wire, cable etc.; optical fibre cables	0.5	0.6	0.6	0.7	0.8	0.9	0.7
Automotive products	4.3	5.8	7.9	9.9	10.6	9.3	10.2
7812 Motor vehicles for the transport of persons, n.e.s.	2.8	4.1	6.3	7.2	8.0	7.1	7.7
7821 Goods vehicles	0.7	0.7	0.7	0.9	1.1	0.9	1.0
Other transport equipment	3.9	2.6	1.6	2.8	1.3	1.4	1.1
Textiles	0.9	0.7	0.7	1.2	1.5	1.4	1.2
Clothing	0.4	0.6	1.5	1.4	2.0	1.8	2.3
8458 Other garments, not knitted or crocheted	0.0	0.1	0.1	0.1	0.1	0.1	0.7
Other consumer goods	6.7	6.1	6.0	7.4	8.0	7.4	7.3
8215 Furniture, n.e.s., of wood	0.5	0.4	0.4	0.5	0.7	0.6	0.6
Other	0.4	0.4	1.7	1.6	2.2	5.2	0.6

Source: UNSD Comtrade database, SITC Rev.3.

Table AI.3
Merchandise exports by destination, 2002-08
(US$ million and per cent)

	2002	2003	2004	2005	2006	2007	2008
Total exports (US$ million)	346.3	465.3	648.8	866.2	991.5	1,232.9	1,497.5
				(Per cent of total)			
America	4.2	4.2	3.9	8.1	12.6	20.1	19.9
United States	3.9	3.3	3.3	3.1	5.9	12.1	6.8
Other America	0.3	0.9	0.6	5.0	6.6	7.9	13.1
Canada	0.0	0.0	0.6	4.1	4.9	5.7	8.8
Mexico	0.0	0.0	0.0	0.4	0.5	1.0	3.5
Europe	42.3	43.1	41.0	39.6	39.4	36.5	40.0
EC(27)	18.4	17.8	19.8	25.0	25.8	21.8	22.3
Bulgaria	0.0	0.0	2.4	4.9	6.3	4.8	7.1
United Kingdom	9.5	6.0	4.9	3.7	2.5	1.9	2.9
France	0.9	1.1	1.5	1.3	3.1	0.9	2.7
Germany	1.6	2.1	2.5	3.3	4.6	4.6	2.2
Spain	0.2	1.5	1.5	1.6	1.7	1.2	1.3
Italy	2.2	1.9	1.8	3.9	2.4	1.4	1.1
Romania	0.0	0.2	0.2	1.0	0.6	0.6	0.9
Netherlands	1.3	2.1	1.5	1.3	0.7	1.0	0.8
EFTA	7.0	7.1	2.8	0.4	0.2	0.1	0.1
Other Europe	16.9	18.1	18.4	14.2	13.4	14.6	17.7
Turkey	15.5	17.7	18.3	14.1	12.6	13.9	17.6
Commonwealth of Independent States[a] (CIS)	48.7	49.1	50.7	47.1	39.8	37.5	36.2
Azerbaijan	8.5	3.6	3.9	9.6	9.3	11.1	13.7
Ukraine	3.7	6.5	2.4	4.3	5.7	7.6	9.0
Armenia	5.8	6.6	8.4	4.6	7.4	9.0	8.3
Russian Federation	17.7	18.0	16.1	17.8	7.6	3.7	1.9
Kazakhstan	0.9	0.9	1.2	1.1	1.6	2.8	1.5
Belarus	0.7	0.4	0.4	0.3	0.3	0.4	0.7
Other CIS	11.6	13.1	18.4	9.4	7.8	2.8	1.1
Africa	0.8	0.0	0.4	1.6	1.4	0.4	0.1
Middle East	2.0	1.2	1.5	1.2	3.5	3.4	1.8
United Arab Emirates	0.6	0.2	0.4	0.5	2.3	1.5	0.7
Iran Islamic Republic	1.0	0.7	0.7	0.5	0.3	0.5	0.6
Asia	1.9	2.4	2.6	2.4	2.6	2.1	1.8
China	0.3	0.3	0.5	0.6	1.0	0.7	0.6
Japan	0.2	0.0	0.1	0.2	0.1	0.0	0.0
Six East Asian Traders	0.5	0.5	0.6	1.1	0.2	0.4	0.5
Other Asia	0.8	1.6	1.4	0.5	1.3	1.0	0.7
India	0.6	1.4	0.9	0.3	0.9	0.7	0.6
Other	0.0	0.0	0.0	0.0	0.0	0.0	0.2

a   Commonwealth of Independent States comprises Armenia, Azerbaijan, Belarus, Georgia, Kazakhstan, Kyrgyzstan, Moldova, Russian Federation, Tajikistan, Turkmenistan, Ukraine, and Uzbekistan.

Source: UNSD, Comtrade database.

Table AI.4
Merchandise imports by origin, 2002-08
(US$ million and per cent)

	2002	2003	2004	2005	2006	2007	2008
Total imports (US$ million)	793.3	1,140.9	1,847.0	2,490.9	3,674.5	5,214.1	6,055.7
				(Per cent of total)			
America	12.2	9.6	8.2	8.0	5.6	5.9	6.3
United States	8.7	8.0	6.0	6.0	3.5	3.9	4.0
Other America	3.5	1.6	2.2	2.1	2.0	2.0	2.4
Brazil	2.3	1.0	1.3	1.3	1.4	1.6	1.7
Europe	45.7	51.8	49.0	43.9	45.8	44.9	43.8
EC(27)	31.3	40.3	36.2	31.5	30.0	29.5	27.4
Germany	7.3	7.2	8.2	8.3	9.6	7.4	7.1
Italy	5.3	3.2	3.3	2.6	2.8	2.8	3.0
Netherlands	1.9	2.1	1.9	2.1	2.0	2.0	2.1
Bulgaria	1.7	1.7	2.1	2.9	3.1	3.5	2.0
France	2.0	4.9	3.4	3.9	1.9	1.9	1.5
Romania	0.7	0.9	0.8	1.6	1.1	1.7	1.5
United Kingdom	3.4	12.8	9.3	2.8	1.7	1.4	1.4
Austria	1.4	1.0	1.2	0.8	0.9	1.0	1.1
Czech Republic	0.7	0.5	0.7	0.8	1.2	1.0	1.0
Greece	1.1	0.8	0.8	0.7	0.6	1.0	0.9
EFTA	2.5	1.5	1.6	0.8	1.0	1.3	1.2
Switzerland	2.3	1.3	1.4	0.7	0.9	1.2	1.1
Other Europe	11.9	10.0	11.2	11.6	14.8	14.1	15.3
Turkey	11.3	9.8	10.9	11.4	14.2	14.0	15.1
Commonwealth of Independent States[a] (CIS)	36.9	32.4	35.6	40.1	38.1	35.5	33.0
Ukraine	7.4	7.0	7.7	8.8	8.7	11.0	10.8
Azerbaijan	10.1	8.2	8.5	9.4	8.7	7.3	10.0
Russian Federation	15.4	14.1	14.0	15.4	15.2	11.1	7.0
Turkmenistan	1.8	0.9	1.8	3.8	2.8	2.9	2.2
Armenia	1.2	1.0	1.4	1.6	1.1	1.1	1.2
Kazakhstan	0.7	0.8	1.2	0.5	0.7	1.2	0.9
Africa	0.2	0.0	0.5	0.2	0.3	0.6	0.7
Middle East	2.1	2.6	3.8	4.5	4.8	5.9	6.2
United Arab Emirates	0.8	1.7	2.5	2.9	3.0	4.1	4.5
Asia	2.9	3.4	2.9	3.3	5.3	7.0	9.3
China	1.1	2.0	1.6	1.9	2.8	4.0	4.9
Japan	0.5	0.2	0.3	0.3	1.1	1.1	1.6
Six East Asian Traders	0.2	0.3	0.4	0.5	0.7	1.0	1.8
Other Asia	1.0	0.9	0.6	0.6	0.7	1.0	1.0
Other	0.1	0.1	0.1	0.0	0.0	0.0	0.6

a   Commonwealth of Independent States comprises Armenia, Azerbaijan, Belarus, Georgia, Kazakhstan, Kyrgyzstan, Moldova, Russian Federation, Tajikistan, Turkmenistan, Ukraine, and Uzbekistan.

Source: UNSD, Comtrade database.

Table AI.5
Trade in services, 2002-08
(US$ million)

	2002	2003	2004	2005	2006	2007	2008
Service balance	44.9	61.2	69.6	83.5	158.0	161.3	22.8
Exports	408.4	458.0	554.8	715.0	885.0	1,094.1	1,260.4
Transportation	200.7	213.4	266.0	331.8	410.8	511.4	613.6
Passenger	17.7	24.7	32.1	45.5	48.0	56.0	57.9
Freight	138.5	139.9	150.0	174.1	227.0	307.5	430.1
Other	44.5	48.8	83.9	112.1	135.8	147.9	125.6
Sea transport	38.1	41.6	61.3	75.2	94.9	109.7	84.5
Passenger	0.6	0.6	0.8	1.3	1.9	1.8	1.1
Freight	0.7	1.1	2.1	3.9	5.3	5.5	5.9
Other	36.7	39.8	58.4	70.0	87.6	102.4	77.5
Air transport	20.2	28.2	51.0	76.6	83.5	83.4	82.9
Passenger	14.5	21.6	28.8	40.0	39.6	43.7	43.6
Freight	0.0	0.0	0.0	0.6	0.9	1.7	1.4
Other	5.8	6.6	22.2	35.9	43.0	38.0	37.9
Other transport	142.4	143.6	153.7	180.0	232.5	318.3	446.2
Pipeline transport and electricity transmission	47.0	47.7	51.0	55.0	90.8	167.0	268.8
Travel	125.7	147.1	176.6	241.4	312.6	383.7	446.6
Business	73.9	87.3	105.4	143.3	167.7	210.2	257.8
Personal	51.8	59.8	71.2	98.1	144.9	173.5	188.9
Communication	17.5	24.2	17.7	19.8	17.5	14.5	23.6
Postal and courier services	1.1	1.1	1.3	1.3	1.3	1.4	1.7
Telecommunication services	16.4	23.1	16.4	18.5	16.3	13.1	22.0
Construction	0.0	0.0	0.0	0.0	0.0	2.8	2.2
Insurance	9.3	9.5	10.0	11.0	13.4	13.0	15.1
Financial (other than insurance)	8.0	10.3	17.4	20.3	18.9	9.1	9.7
Computer and information	0.0	0.0	0.0	0.1	0.5	1.9	3.5
Royalties and license fees	5.5	6.3	7.7	9.3	12.9	10.6	6.2
Other business services	3.7	7.4	10.6	10.8	8.8	20.3	27.1
Personal, cultural and recreational services	0.1	0.2	2.1	3.2	5.5	8.7	9.0
Government services, n.i.e.	37.9	39.5	46.6	67.4	84.1	118.0	103.8
Imports	-363.4	-396.7	-485.1	-631.5	-727.0	-932.8	-1,237.7
Transportation debit	-109	-137.2	-205.5	-288.0	-387.8	-507.3	-642.0
Passenger	-40	-40.3	-48.9	-68.5	-90.2	-101.1	-134.3
Freight	-57	-83.5	-139.7	-192.0	-272.1	-381.3	-480.6
Other	-11	-13.3	-16.9	-27.6	-25.4	-24.9	-27.1
Sea transport	-24	-37.4	-65.9	-81.2	-104.7	-146.6	-181.4
Passenger	-0.8	-0.8	-0.7	-0.8	-0.9	-0.5	-0.7
Freight	-21.0	-34.2	-62.1	-75.9	-97.6	-140.6	-175.6
Other	-2.6	-2.5	-3.1	-4.5	-6.2	-5.5	-5.1
Air transport	-48	-50.4	-64.2	-92.2	-105.0	-131.2	-158.8
Passenger	-31.8	-31.4	-38.1	-51.5	-60.0	-65.6	-90.1
Freight	-8.8	-10.2	-15.0	-22.7	-30.1	-52.4	-55.4
Other	-7.2	-8.9	-11.1	-18.0	-14.9	-13.2	-13.3
Other transport	-36	-49.3	-75.4	-114.6	-178.1	-229.6	-301.8
Travel	-148.9	-130.2	-147.4	-168.8	-166.6	-175.8	-203.5
Business	-79.3	-69.7	-101.7	-111.0	-112.6	-115.9	-147.5
Personal	-69.6	-60.5	-45.6	-57.8	-54.1	-59.9	-55.9
Communication	-10.5	-15.8	-13.3	-17.3	-14.4	-11.4	-13.1
Postal and courier services	-0.2	-0.3	-0.4	-0.5	-0.4	-0.5	-0.5
Telecommunication services	-10.3	-15.5	-13.0	-16.9	-14.0	-10.9	-12.6
Construction	-14.5	-14.9	-7.1	-16.0	-4.3	-6.2	-17.8
Insurance	-18.0	-27.9	-42.3	-58.9	-80.4	-110.8	-150.7
Financial (other than insurance)	-2.8	-2.0	-2.6	-2.2	-4.2	-12.1	-16.1
Computer and information	-0.5	-0.7	-0.7	-1.1	-0.8	-2.3	-10.6
Royalties and license fees	-10.7	-10.6	-5.7	-5.3	-5.0	-4.9	-8.4
Other business services	-9.0	-15.8	-15.1	-26.1	-23.7	-34.8	-74.2
Personal, cultural and recreational services	0.0	0.0	0.0	0.0	0.0	-6.7	-17.9
Government services, n.i.e.	-39.9	-41.8	-45.5	-47.6	-39.9	-60.6	-83.4

Source: National Bank of Georgia online information. Viewed at: http://www.nbg.gov.ge/index.php?m=306&lng=eng# external [8 June 2009].

Table AII.1
Heritage Foundation 2009 Index of Economic Freedom

Georgia's economic freedom score is 69.8, making its economy the 32nd freest (out of 179) in the 2009 Index, shifting from 96th place in 2005 and from "mostly unfree" to "mostly free". Georgia has made great progress in liberating its citizens from economic constraints but is still below world averages in property rights and freedom from corruption.

Labour Freedom 99.4: Highly flexible labour regulations enhance employment opportunities and productivity growth. Rules on the number of work hours are very flexible. The non-salary cost of employing a worker can be moderate, and dismissing a redundant employee is costless.

Fiscal Freedom 86.8: Georgia has a moderate income tax and a low corporate tax. The top income tax rate is a flat 25%, and the corporate tax rate is 15%, down from 20% as of January 2008. Other taxes include a value-added tax (VAT), a tax on interest, and a tax on dividends. In the most recent year, overall tax revenue as a percentage of GDP was 21.7%.

Business Freedom 86.6: Starting a business takes an average of three days, compared to the world average of 38 days. Obtaining a business licence requires less than the world average of 18 procedures and 225 days. Closing a business is relatively simple.

Trade Freedom 80.6: Georgia has made significant progress toward liberalizing its trade regime, but some import restrictions, agriculture subsidies, some import and export licensing, and inadequate infrastructure and trade capacity still add to the cost of trade. Some border trade goes unreported.

Monetary Freedom 70.9: Inflation is relatively high, averaging 9.1% between 2005 and 2007. Prices are generally set in the market, but the Government may impose controls through state-owned enterprises. It also provides subsidies for agricultural products and energy, which distort domestic prices.

Investment Freedom 70.0: Foreign and domestic investments receive equal treatment. Exceptions may be made for investments in certain sectors, including maritime fisheries, air and maritime transport, and broadcasting. The State retains a controlling interest in air traffic control, shipping traffic control, railroad control systems, defence and weapons industries, and nuclear energy. Foreign firms may participate freely in privatizations, though transparency has been an issue. Residents and non-residents may hold foreign exchange accounts. Foreign individuals and companies may buy non-agricultural land. Only domestic entities may buy agricultural land, but agricultural land can be purchased by forming a Georgian corporation that may be up to 100% foreign-owned.

Financial Freedom 60.0: Georgia's financial sector has undergone substantial liberalization. Beginning in the 1990s, the central bank assumed a supervisory role and imposed stringent reporting and capital requirements that led to the closure or merging of a number of banks. Loans to the private sector have increased rapidly in recent years. Foreign bank branches and subsidiaries are welcome to operate in Georgia, and there are no formal or effective barriers. The Government does not have a financial stake in any bank although the stock exchange is small and underdeveloped. In March 2008, Parliament approved the Global Competitiveness of the Financial Services Sector Act to enhance the sector's efficiency.

Property Rights 35.0: Judicial corruption is still a problem despite substantial improvement in efficiency and fairness in the courts. Both foreigners and Georgians continue to doubt the judicial system's ability to protect private property and contracts. The enforcement of laws protecting intellectual property rights is weak.

Freedom From Corruption 34.0: Corruption is perceived as significant. Georgia ranks 79th out of 179 countries in Transparency International's Corruption Perceptions Index for 2007. The Government has improved its performance in fighting corruption; it has fired thousands of civil servants and police, and several high-level officials have been prosecuted for corruption-related offences.

Source: Heritage Foundation (2009), *The 2009 Index of Economic Freedom.*   Viewed at: http://www.heritage.org/ index/Country/Georgia.

Table AII.2
Selected notifications to the WTO, 2002-09

WTO Agreement	Description of requirement	Periodicity	Most recent notification	Comment
Agriculture				
Article 18.2	Export subsidies	Annual	G/AG/N/GEO/6, 24 June 2005	No export subsidies for the calendar year 2004
Article 18.2 DS:1	Domestic support		G/AG/N/ GEO/7, 13 July 2007	List of DS measures notifications calendar year 2004
General Agreement on Trade in Services				
Article III:4 or IV:2	Enquiry point	Once, then changes	S/ENQ/78/Rev.9, 1 December 2006	Division of Multilateral Economic Cooperation, at MFA
GATT Article XXIV:7(a)p GATS Article V:7(a)	RTA		WT/REG261/N/1, 24 February 2009	Georgia - Turkey Free Trade Agreement
Agreement on the Implementation of Article VI				
Article 18.5 GATT 1994 Article VI	Laws and regulations	Once, then changes	G/ADP/N/1/GEO/1, 6 February 2002	No notification of laws/regulations
Agreement on Implementation of Article VII				
Article 22	Customs valuation	Once	G/VAL/N/1/GEO/1, 22 April 2002	Regulations concerning order of determining the customs value of goods imported to Georgia
GATT 1994				
Article XVII:4(a))	State Trading Enterprises	Annual	G/STR/N/7-8/GEO, 16 September 2002	State trading activities
Import Licensing				
Article 1.4(a) & 8.2 (b)	Import licensing laws and regulations	Once, then changes	G/LIC/N/1/GEO/1, 8 April 2002	Notification on import licensing procedures
Article 7.3	Import licensing	Once, then changes	G/LIC/N/3/GEO/3, 4 September 2006	Response to Questionnaire on Import Licensing Procedures (G/LIC/3)
Preshipment Inspection				
Article 5	Laws and regulations	Once, then changes	G/PSI/N/1/Add.10, 19 July 2004	See Article 176 of Customs Code of Georgia - not compulsory
Market Access	Notification procedures quantitative restrictions	Every two years from 31 January 1996	G/MA/NTM/QR/1/Add.10, 28 March 2006	Quantitave restrictions (2004)
Rules of Origin				
Articles 5 & 4			G/RO/N/37, 3 June 2002	Rules of origin on imported goods
Subsidies and Countervailing Measures				
			G/RO/N/38, 7 October 2002	Rules on determining country of origin in FTA between CIS countries
Article 25	Subsidies	Annual	G/SCM/N/123/GEO, 14 June 2005	No specific subsidies granted for the calendar year 2004
Article 25.11	Countervailing measures	Semi-annual	G/SCM/N/138/Add.1/Rev.1, 18 October 2006	No countervailing action during 1 July to 31 December 2005
Article 32.6			G/SCM/N/1/GEO, 6 February 2002	No law regulating countervailing measures
Safeguards				
Articles 12.6	Safeguards	Once, then changes	G/SG/N/1/GEO/1, 7 February 2002	No law regulating safeguard measures

Table AII.2 (cont'd)

WTO Agreement	Description of requirement	Periodicity	Most recent notification	Comment
Sanitary and Phytosanitary Measures				
Article 7 Annex B	Sanitary and phytosanitary measures	Ad hoc	G/SPS/N/GEO/18-22, latest notification dated 13 October 2003	Plant protection and animal health measures
Technical Barriers to Trade				
Annex 3C	Code of Good Practices		G/TBT/CS/N/153, 17 December 2003	State Department of Standardization, Metrology and Certification (GEOSTAND)
Article 15.2	Implementation & administration of the Agreement		G/TBT/2/Add.81, 15 October 2004	Law of Georgia on Standardization and on Certification of Products and Services (GEOSTAND)
Article 2.9	Notifications		G/TBT/N/GEO/3 – 5, 19 January 2004	Adoption of international & regional standards
Article 5.6	Notifications		G/TBT/N/GEO/1 – 2, 5 August 2003	Notification of technical regulations
Trade-Related Investment Measures				
Article 6.2	Investment		G/TRIMS/N/2/Rev.9/Add.3, 21 March 2002	Georgia does not maintain any TRIMs
Trade-Related Aspects of Intellectual Property Rights				
TRIPS Article 63.2	Copyright and neighbouring rights	Once, then changes	IP/N/1/GEO/1, 30 August 2002	Main IPR laws: copyright, trade marks, GIs, industrial design, patents, layout designs of integrated circuits, protection of undisclosed information, and border enforcement
Article 69	Contact points	Once, then changes	IP/N/3/Rev.6/Add.1, 24 July 2002	Georgian National Intellectual Property Centre: Sakpatenti
Government Procurement			GPA/68, 14 May 2002	Legislations in the field of Government Procurement

Source: WTO documents.

Table AIII.1

Key problems and recommendations after three years of licensing reform

Problems	Recommendations	Expected impact
- Silence is consent principle is not fully applied in issuance of licences/permits - There are contradictory clauses in the framework law on licenses and permits (Article 16 and 32)	- The scope of application of silence is consent principle to be determined - Detailed procedures for silence is consent application should be formulated - Changes to the law on licenses and permits should be passed with the aim to eliminate contradictions between silence is consent principle and specific rules set by Articles 16 and 32 of the framework law in favour of silence is consent principle	- Full-scale and effective application of silence is consent principle by licence/permit seekers - Establishment of reciprocal and accountable public services in administrative bodies that would strictly meet deadlines set by the law
- Although one-stop-shop principle is in place, in a number of cases applicants still have to collect documents, get approvals from various administrative bodies, and run from one institution to another to obtain seals and signatures	- Licensing bodies should implement one-stop-shop principle and restructure their corresponding services in a way that guarantees strict adherence to deadlines and frees applicants from the obligation to collect documents, seals, and signatures by themselves - Amend the framework law in a way that guarantees applicants' interaction with only a single agency - Clearly fix responsibility of issuing administrative body for any and all necessary coordination with other governmental agencies	- Applicants will only interact with a single administrative body - Licensing bodies will provide better quality service in less time - Licensing process will be less time- and cost-demanding for applicants
- Respective legislation is fragmented: Framework law Governmental resolutions Ministerial orders - Respective legislation is subject to frequent changes	- Sector-by-sector laws should be passed - Determine frequency of possible changes to laws/ governmental resolutions/ministerial orders per year - Changes to legislation should enter into force after 3-6 months following their promulgation	- Sector-by-sector laws will clearly define responsibilities and strict timeframes for fulfilling the responsibilities of issuing administrative agencies - Changes will happen less frequently - Public will have enough time to raise awareness of new laws
- Some procedural requirements of the framework law are not met according to schedule: Sector-by-sector laws have not been passed The framework law is not safe of amending with new licences/permits There is no governmental body ensuring periodical critical review of the list of licences/permits or the list of required documentation	- Determine central governmental body responsible for each component of the framework law - Periodically review of the list of licences/permits with the aim to further reduce their number where appropriate - Periodically review the list of required documentation and approvals - Carry out periodical regulatory impact assessments for businesses	- Clearly defined state policy guaranteeing permanent progress in regulation of licence/permit sphere - Reduced ability of state agencies to circumvent reforms with additional licences/permits
- Law does not specify licence/ permit issuing administrative bodies	- The list of licences/permits in the law should be amended with the list of corresponding issuing administrative bodies - Law should contain detailed description of each secondary agency's scope of authority	- Direct linkage between framework law and implementing secondary legislation - Simplified application process for entrepreneurs

Source: International Finance Corporation (2008), *Georgia: After Three Years of Licensing Reform – Analytical Note*, p. 4. Viewed at: http://www.ifc.org/ifcext/georgiasme.nsf/AttachmentsByTitle/LicensingPolicyPaperEng/$FILE/ LicensingPolicyPaper.pdf.

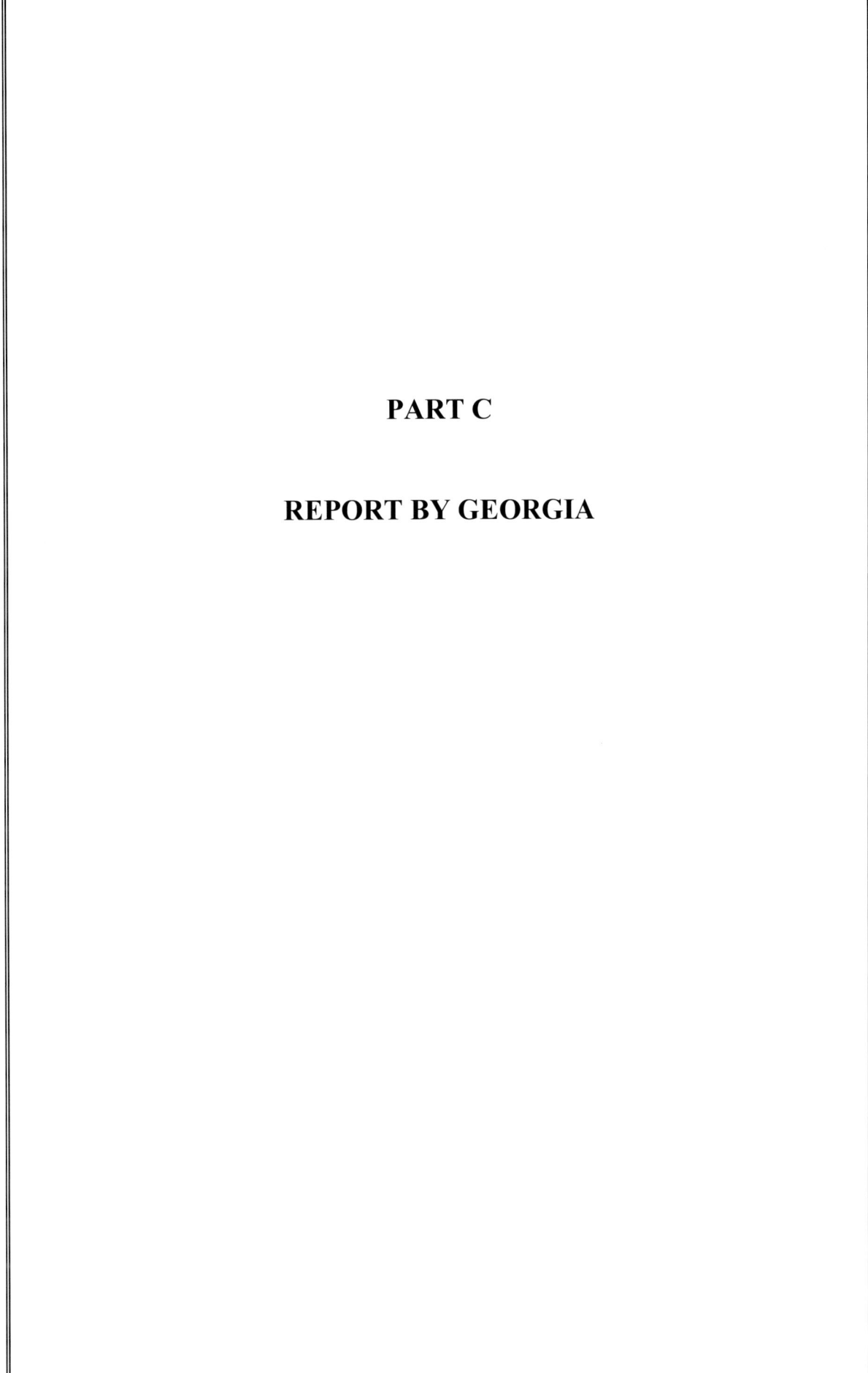

PART C

REPORT BY GEORGIA

CONTENTS

1. INTRODUCTION

1. Trade liberalization is one of the key objectives on Georgia's economic policy agenda. In the reporting period Georgia undertook a large number of reform initiatives targeted at streamlining, liberalization and simplification of trade regulations and their implementation. This effort has been particularly intensified after the Rose Revolution of November 2003. Starting from 2004 Georgia almost entirely eliminated tariff barriers and drastically reduced non-tariff barriers to trade. Domestic trade related legislation was brought in conformity with WTO standards. These reforms contributed to the creation of competitive market conditions and business enabling environment, diversified international trade and economic ties and thus generated growth and development.

2. Economic and trade reforms were embedded in a coherent and intensive reform program of the new Government after the Rose Revolution, whereby the following inter-related key priorities were identified:

- Eradication of corruption and red-tape.
- Full introduction of market economy principles.
- Liberal trade reforms and diversification of international economic relations.
- Enhancement of transparency in the policy making process.
- Reduction of the size of bureaucracy and enhancement of professional qualification of civil servants.
- The supremacy of the law and equality of all before the law.
- Protection of human rights and political liberties.

2. RECENT ECONOMIC DEVELOPMENTS AND REFORMS

2.1 Macroeconomic Overview

3. Georgia's economic performance since joining the WTO is impressive. GDP growth has been particularly strong in 2003-2007, averaging nearly 10% annually. FDI has more than doubled from 8.3% of GDP in 2003 to 19.3% in 2007. Sectors that attracted highest shares of investment in 2007-2008 were transport and communications, energy, services, manufacturing and construction. The openness rate i.e. share of foreign trade in the GDP reached 60% in 2008 compared to 40% in 2003. Public debt has been reduced from 56% of GDP in 2003 to 25.5% in 2007. Budget revenues increased five times, although taxes were drastically reduced.

4. Despite the August 2008 war with Russia and the following Global Financial Crisis Georgia's economy remained resilient and continued to grow in 2008 although at a lower rate than previously. GDP grew at 2.1% in 2008. GDP per capita amounted to 2,920$ in 2008. Projected economic growth for 2009 is -1.5%. This is a relatively good result compared to other economies of similar size and Georgia's regional peers. Three main factors contributed to such remarkable resilience of Georgia's economy:

- Liberal economic policies and market reforms of the past 5 years created an open and diversified economy.
- Banking sector proved to be resilient and maintained stability.
- Unprecedented international support of US$4.5 billion pledged at the Brussels Donor Conference in October 2008 kept foreign inflows in Georgia and contributed to the stability of the economy.

5.   The Government prepared a special Strategy to deal with the Global Financial Crisis, which helped Georgia to minimize the negative affect of the crisis. The Strategy includes the Economic Stimulus Package ($2.2 bln) and the Social Assistance Package ($1.6 bln).

6.   Under the Economic Stimulus Package the Government initiated further tax cuts in order to stimulate demand and increase private spending as an additional tool for avoiding significant decrease of economic activity. Income tax was reduced from 25% to 20% from January 1, 2009 and it will be further decreased to 15% by 2012. In addition $1.95 bln is being invested in infrastructure projects in order to help stimulate growth and employment.

7.   Social Assistance Package envisages increased assistance to the socially needy which among others includes rising of pensions, salaries (in education sector), cash benefits to the population living under poverty line and coverage of state insurance programs.

8.   Liberal economic reforms and improved business environment have been well reflected in various international ratings. Georgia's rating in the Ease of Doing Business 2010 Survey was further improved from 15 to 11. This means that according to the World Bank and IFC, Georgia is eleventh the most attractive place to do business worldwide. This is up from 112th in 2005. In addition, the World Bank proclaimed Georgia as Europe and Central Asia's top Doing Business reformer over the past five years in the 2009 survey.

9.   In particular, according to the Ease of Doing Business 2010, Georgia is the 2nd best worldwide in registering property, 5th – in starting a business, 7th – in dealing with construction licenses and 9th – in employing workers.

2.2   Regulatory Reform and Fight against Corruption

10.   In order to stimulate private sector development and minimize public sector involvement in economic processes, the post-Rose Revolution reform agenda of the Georgian Government has put a special emphasis on the improvement of civil sector performance and the fight against corruption. The objective of the Government is to establish an efficient, professional and transparent public sector.

11.   Institutional reforms in the civil sector have included downsizing and optimization of government structures. All types of duplication of functions have been abolished and lean government structures have been established. In order to reduce corruption and make public sector jobs competitive, salaries have been raised substantially.

12.   In 2005, the system of business licensing was modernized and simplified. A lot of unnecessary regulations, which were the source of corruption, were abolished. The number of licenses and permits necessary for doing business was reduced by almost 85% and a business licensing "One Stop Shop" and "Silence is Consent" principle was introduced.

13.   As a result of changes to the Tax Code and Law on Entrepreneurs in 2005 and 2006, business registration became simple, cheap and efficient, taking only one day for legal entities and individuals to register a company. State and tax registration of companies is now carried out by the Revenue Service of Georgia under one single procedure.

14.   Due to reforms carried out in recent years corruption was largely eradicated in state institutions and civil service. According to the 2009 Corruption Barometer survey by Transparency International – which assesses corruption in the six major institutions in a country: political parties, parliament, business sector, media, civil service and judiciary – Georgia ranks first in the CIS and 6th

in the region (EU, CIS and Western Balkan) on average corruption score for all six institutions. Notably, it ranks on the same level as Norway.

15.   The Survey assesses positively Georgian Government's effort to reduce corruption. 57% of respondents consider Government's actions very effective. It reports that in the survey period only 2% of Georgians surveyed had to pay a bribe. This puts Georgia on the first place in the CIS and in the top five in the region. In a 2009 survey by the International Finance Corporation, only 4% of firms in Georgia said, they expected to make 'informal payments' compared to the average of 32% in Eastern Europe and Central Asia.

2.3   Privatization

16.   The privatization process was launched in Georgia in 1993 and involved mostly small and medium scale entities (commercial, household servicing establishments, drug stores and etc). The most active phase of the privatization process started in 2004. The government opened all sectors of the Georgian economy for privatization, including energy, transport and communications. Almost all major state-run companies have already been privatized. In an effort to attract more foreign investments in the Georgian economy, the Government plans to continue a transparent yet aggressive policy of privatization.

17.   Until 2005, 75% of agricultural land and 2.5 million hectares of forests were under state-ownership. In 2005, the Law on Privatization of State-Owned Agricultural Land was adopted in order to promote efficient use of land through private ownership and thus increase efficiency in the agricultural sector. Forests and other natural resources are being transferred more actively to private hands under long-term tradable licenses.

2.4   Tax and Customs Reform

18.   Since joining the WTO in 2000, Georgia's tax and customs systems have undergone significant reform. The new Tax Code enacted in January 2005 lowered tax rates and simplified the tax system across-the-board. Flat, simple and easy to administer tax system was introduced. Currently there are only 6 taxes instead of the previous 21, namely: the profit, property, income, VAT, excise, and gambling taxes. The income tax is 20% (instead of previous 33%), and will be further reduced to 15% in the coming years, the VAT – 18% (instead of previous 20%), the profit tax – 15% (instead of previous 20%). A large number of taxes were abolished altogether.

19.   In parallel with tax reduction, tax administration improved significantly. As a result, despite drastic tax reductions, tax revenues increased approximately 3 times from 2003 to 2008.

20.   In September 2006 Georgia abolished import duties on almost 90% of goods (except some agricultural products and construction materials) and reduced the number of import duties from 16 to only 3 – 0%, 5% and 12%. This along with attractive business regulations and favourable export regimes helps Georgia to raise its investment attractiveness.

21.   The new Customs Code, which became effective from January 2007, is an important step towards reducing corruption at customs, streamlining customs procedures and bringing them in compliance with international standards. Risk Management System was gradually introduced in all customs units in 2008. From January 1, 2009 risk management system and risk analysis based customs control via ASYCUDA customs declaration processing IT system covers import, export, customs warehouse and part of re-export. All customs check-points were modernized.

2.5 Labour Market Reform

22.   Among the major problems facing Georgia today is unemployment. The Government has taken several initiatives to deal with this problem. In order to legalize labour relations and facilitate job creation a new Labour Code was enacted in 2006, which is in compliance with ILO core standards such as:

- Freedom of association and the right to collective bargaining (C87, C98).
- The elimination of all forms of forced or compulsory labour (C29, C105).
- The abolition of the most hazardous forms of child labour (C138, C182).
- The elimination of discrimination in respect of employment and occupation (C100, C111).

23.   The Labour Code of 2006 replaced the Soviet style labour legislation adopted in the seventies. Recent labour reforms contributed to the creation of a more flexible and dynamic job market.

24.   Apart from this, the system of vocational training was introduced and streamlined on the basis of public private partnership in order to produce a skilled workforce that can be adapted to modern requirements of the labour market.

2.6 Technical Regulation System Reform

25.   Upon entering the WTO, Georgia undertook an obligation to introduce a voluntary system of standards and to decrease the list of goods which are subject to compulsory certification.

26.   In 2005, the Government of Georgia initiated reform of the standardization, metrology and accreditation systems, which was aimed at removal of technical barriers to international trade and ensure transparency in the field of technical regulations. As a result, the institutional and structural arrangement of standardization and accreditation fields was optimized, and a system of accreditation, quality control, standardization and technical regulation was introduced that is compatible with international standards. Also, the system of mandatory standardization was replaced by voluntary standards, and the regulatory function of the state in standardization field was reduced. Bringing Georgia's system of technical regulations in line with international standards has helped to simplify import/export procedures.

27.   In 2006, Georgia accepted and officially allowed the use of technical regulations of over 30 countries, above all of the members of the EU and the Organization of Economic Cooperation and Development (OECD).

28.   This sphere remains under the special attention of the Government in order to bring it in compliance with international standards and thus reduce technical barriers to trade. For this reason the Government recently prepared a Strategy in Standardization, Accreditation, Conformity Assessment, Technical Regulation and Metrology and a Program on Legislative Reform and Adoption of Technical Regulations.

2.7 Infrastructure Development

29.   At the time of joining the WTO, one of the major inhibitors of faster economic growth and productivity in Georgia was lack of infrastructure. This has been well recognized by the new Government after the Rose Revolution and several steps have been taken in order to address the problem, including creation of improved transportation links (roads, railway and port facilities), and continued reform to increase efficiency in power and telecommunications.

30.   The reliability of the Georgian energy system has improved substantially in recent years. Georgia now enjoys a 24 hour a day electricity supply instead of chronic power shortages typical before 2004. As a result of eradicating corruption in this field, revenue collection has been increased drastically from 20% in 2004 to around 95% by 2008. In the past couple of years Georgia turned from a country with semi-permanent black-outs to a net electricity exporter. Today Georgia exports electricity to all its neighbours: Turkey, Azerbaijan, Armenia and Russia.

31.   The Government focused on investments in rehabilitating domestic hydropower plants, strengthening major transmission lines, and enhancing the energy cooperation with neighbouring countries. The key objective of Georgia's policy is to ensure full security of energy supply and demand. As dependence on imports from unreliable suppliers presents a serious risk, Georgia is trying to avoid this problem through the diversification of supply. Today Georgia has three suppliers of gas from three different sources. Development of energy transportation infrastructure is a priority in this regard. Construction of new high voltage transmission lines between Georgia and Turkey will start in the Fall of 2009.

32.   Moreover, the Government is promoting investments in renewable energy, in particular construction of medium and small hydro-power plants to reduce dependency on natural gas in the electricity generation sector. The results were already apparent in late 2006. Rehabilitation of existing hydro plants allowed the power system of Georgia to export power (even during the winter periods), which is unprecedented since the creation of the independent Georgian power system.

33.   With the aim of liberalization of air transport, Georgia pursues 'open sky' policy and on the basis of bilateral agreements with its major partners has abolished restrictions on the number of passengers, destinations and frequency of flights. In road transport, Georgia has liberalized conditions by means of abolishing excessive transit fees, quotas and other transit barriers. In maritime transport the country is focused on diversifying its connections to the West via the Black Sea. In the railway sector, liberalized tariff policy, improved management, and prospective railway projects better connecting Georgia and its regional neighbours, contribute to the increase of country's attractiveness as a transit route from the East to the West. Baku-Tbilisi-Kars railway project, which is scheduled to be completed in 2011, will not only link Georgia, Turkey and Azerbaijan, but is supposed to increase the transportation capacity in the South Caucasus and diversify the nature of the goods that are transported through these three countries.

3.   TRADE POLICY OBJECTIVES AND DEVELOPMENT

34.   Georgia remains strongly committed to the WTO as the primary basis for its trade policy. Georgia firmly believes that the best way to meet challenges facing an increasingly globalised world economy is trade liberalization.

35.   The basic objectives of the trade policy of Georgia are:

-     Integration into the world economy, which implies implementation of obligations undertaken by joining WTO and other international agreements.
-     Trade policy liberalization, including simplification of export and import procedures and tariff and non-tariff regulations.

- Diversification of trade relations by concluding free trade agreements with main trading or regional partners.
- Investment promotion through creation of business friendly environment.

36. Georgia has a very liberal trade regime with simplified trade procedures, no quantitative restrictions on export or import and no tariff quotas. Georgia has one of the lowest tariff rates worldwide. Its average MFN rate is 1.5%. There is effectively no tariff escalation nor any tariff peaks.

37. In accordance with the Georgian legislation no tariff duty is applied to export or re-export from Georgia. Export is exempted from VAT as well. Georgia does not use minimum export prices and export subsidies.

38. There are no non-tariff restrictions (prohibitions, licensing) in international trade included in the Georgian legislation except those cases where health, security, safety and environmental issues are concerned. The share of goods subject to non-tariff restrictions constitutes about 1% of the whole nomenclature.

3.1   Facts on Trade

39. Due to the reforms carried out by the Government of Georgia in 2003-2008 the barriers to foreign trade decreased tremendously, resulting in increased volumes of export and import flows. Whereas in 2000-2002 the average annual growth of trade turnover was 7.2%, this figure increased substantially in 2003-2008 and constituted 38.8%.

40. In 2003-2008 import grew at an average rate of 43% and reached US$6,058.1 mln in 2008. Main import products are petroleum oils and gases, motor cars, medicines and different machinery. In the same period export grew at an average rate of 28% and reached US$1,497.7 mln in 2008. Traditionally main export products of Georgia have been agricultural products (mineral waters, wine, nuts, citrus). The structure of Georgia's export has changed in recent years and besides agricultural products is constituted of ferroalloys, copper ores, fertilizers, gold.

41. Historically the Russian Federation was Georgia's number one trade partner, with a share averaging 17% of total trade turnover. As a result of the Russian embargo on Georgian exports, which started in 2005 and still continues, total trade between the two countries decreased substantially. Turkey is now Georgia's top trade partner, followed by Azerbaijan and Ukraine.

42. The share of EU countries in Georgia's total trade turnover have been increasing year by year and amounted to 27% in 2008. Among top ten trade partners there are three EU members: Germany, Bulgaria and Italy.

3.2   Trade Agreements and Arrangements

(a)   World Trade Organization

43. The entry of Georgia into the WTO on June 14th, 2000 was a significant step towards integration into world trade. Georgia became the 137th member country. It was the fourth former Soviet republic to become a member government of the WTO (after the Kyrgyz Republic, Latvia and Estonia). Upon its entry into the WTO, Georgia was granted the Most Favourable Nation (MFN) treatment by all WTO member states and it conferred MFN in return.

44.   Georgia is a party to all WTO agreements except the Government Procurement Agreement (GPA). Nevertheless, a Law on Government Procurement which is in compliance with the WTO requirements has been in force since 2006. Thus, Georgia is ready to join the GPA in the near future.

(b)   CIS Free Trade Agreement

45.   Georgia has been a party to the Commonwealth of Independent States (CIS) multilateral agreement on the creation of a free trade zone since April 15th, 1994. The agreement was ratified by all CIS member countries except Russia. The agreement became the basis for the bilateral Free trade Agreements between CIS countries. Georgia has eight bilateral FTAs with Azerbaijan, Turkmenistan, Armenia, Ukraine, Kazakhstan, Moldova, Uzbekistan (not yet ratified) and Russia.

46.   Protocols on exceptions from free trade were concluded only with the Russian Federation and Kazakhstan. Later in 2004, according to the bilateral negotiations in the framework of Kazakhstan's accession to the WTO, parties abolished the protocol.

(c)   Free Trade Agreement with Turkey

47.   Turkey has been Georgia's largest trading partner since 2006. Negotiations on concluding a free trade agreement started in January 2007 and in November 2007 a free trade agreement between Georgia and the Republic of Turkey was signed. It came into force from November 1, 2008. According to this agreement, customs tariffs on industrial products have been fully eliminated. Meanwhile, some agricultural products are subject to tariff quotas.

(d)   GUAM Free Trade Agreement

48.   GUAM is a regional organization of four states (Georgia, Ukraine, Azerbaijan and Moldova). For a short period of time (1999-2002), the organization was named GUUAM due to the membership of Uzbekistan, which then withdrew from the organization and it was renamed GUAM.

49.   The Free Trade Agreement, which was concluded in the framework of this organization in 2002, is more liberal than CIS Free Trade Agreement and does not envisage any exceptions from a free trade.

(e)   European Union

50.   In foreign trade activities of Georgia, one of the priority directions is the trade relations with the European Union. The basis and legal foundation for EU-Georgia relations is the Partnership and Cooperation Agreement (PCA) which was negotiated while Georgia was going through the process of WTO integration and concluded on the 22nd of April 1996. It entered into force in 1999. The agreement aims to foster cooperation, not only in trade issues, but also in political, environmental and cultural areas.

51.   The EU-Georgia European Neighbourhood Policy Action Plan, signed in November 2006, envisages further enhancement of bilateral trade relations including possible establishment of a Free Trade Agreement between the EU and Georgia. In this context the EU Commission has launched the EU-Georgia FTA Feasibility Study, which concluded that having a Deep and Comprehensive Free Trade Agreement (DCFTA) between the two countries is mutually beneficial. Intensive bilateral consultations with the EU and preparatory works for the future DCFTA negotiations have already started.

52.   The EU-Georgia bilateral negotiations on the Agreement on Protection of Geographical Indications for Agricultural Products and other Foodstuff is almost finalized and is expected to be signed in the first half of 2010.

53.   Georgia actively participates in a new Eastern Partnership initiative of European Union. In December 2008 the European Commission announced plans to enhance its relationship with Georgia (as well as Armenia, Azerbaijan, Moldova, Ukraine) as part of a new Eastern Partnership Initiative that would involve the gradual integration into the EU economy for Eastern Partnership countries that were willing and able to enter into a deeper engagement. The initiative envisages signing of Association Agreements with partner countries.

54.   For Georgia, like other countries with a transition economy, the opportunity to use the Generalized System of Preference (GSP), has been of crucial importance. It has provided a preferential tariff mode for production imported from Georgia. Since 1995 Georgia has benefited from the scheme of GSP granted by the EU. In 2005, the EU provided Georgia with an expanded opportunity to make use of tariff privileges (GSP+) that consists of granting a trade regime without duties on the import of approximately 7,200 products.

(f)   United States

55.   In June 2007, Georgia and the United States signed a Trade and Investment Framework Agreement (TIFA). The TIFA sets up a joint U.S.-Georgia Council on Trade and Investment that addresses a wide range of trade and investment issues including trade capacity building, intellectual property, labour, and environmental issues. The Council will also help to increase commercial and investment opportunities by identifying and working to remove impediments to trade and investment flows between the United States and Georgia.

56.   It is noteworthy to mention that according to the US-Georgia Charter of Strategic Partnership signed on 9 January 2009, Georgia and the United States will explore the possibility of a Free Trade Agreement.

(g)   Black Sea Economic Cooperation (BSEC) Organization

57.   In accordance with the founding document, 12 member countries of the Organization of Black Sea Economic Cooperation (BSEC) collaborate in the various spheres such as trade and economic cooperation, banking, agriculture, healthcare and pharmaceuticals, environmental protection, tourism, science and technology, information exchange in various sectors.

58.   The share of Georgia's trade volume with BSEC countries constitutes around 53%.

(h)   Other Agreements and Arrangements

59.   Georgia has established a legal framework for cooperation with many countries. It has developed and signed bilateral agreements on trade and economic cooperation with 46 countries.

60.   Georgia has joined many multilateral trading agreements and international conventions. Among them the following basic important documents should be mentioned:

-     The Paris Convention on Protection of the Industrial Property
-     The Madrid Agreement on Registration of Trading Trade-Marks
-     The Agreement on Protection of Patents
-     The Viennese Convention on Contracts of Sale and Purchase of Goods.

61. Under the Generalized System of Preferences Georgia receives preferential access to the markets of the EU (GSP+), the United States, Canada, Japan, Switzerland and Norway.

3.3 Investment Policy

62. There has been a broad consensus in Georgia regarding its integration into the international economy through opening up of the Georgian economy for business activities and creation of a favourable investment environment. Georgia started market oriented reforms in 1995. National treatment is applied to all investors and there is no specific regulation that foresees discrimination. All sectors of the Georgian economy are open for investments.

63. The Law of Georgia on the Investment Activity Promotion and Guarantees, which has been in place since 1996, defines the legal basis for realizing both foreign and local investments and their protection guarantees on the territory of Georgia. The purpose of the Law is to establish investment enabling environment. It secures equal treatment and rights to Georgian and foreign investors.

64. The Law on State Support for Investments was adopted in 2006, with the aim to further optimize procedures necessary for investing and entrepreneurial activities.

65. Georgia has signed bilateral investment promotion and protection agreements with 30 countries and agreements on avoidance of double taxation with 26 countries.

66. The foreign direct investment (FDI) promotion is the responsibility of the Georgian National Investment Agency (GNIA) under the Ministry of Economic Development. GNIA acts as a 'one-stop shop' agency for investors, assisting them in setting up their businesses in Georgia, helping in project implementation, performing a liaison role with the Government, providing information on investment opportunities in the country, as well as investment related regulations and laws.

67. In its export promotion activities, GNIA helps to find markets for products, undertakes market studies and seeks out partners for joint ventures aimed at increasing the volume of exports and development of Georgian enterprises. GNIA organizes international conferences, business-forums, trade fairs and exhibitions.

4. CONCLUSIONS

68. To summarize, in the reporting period Georgia undertook intensive trade liberalization effort. As a result of consequent and coherent reform measures, tariff and non-tariff barriers to trade were largely eliminated, export and import procedures were simplified and trade flows were increased and diversified.

69. Trade related reforms are part of the overall economic reform agenda vigorously pursued by the Government since the Rose Revolution.

70. Streamlined business and trade regulations contributed to substantial diversification to Georgia's international economic relations, including trade and investment, which in turn made Georgia's economy extremely resilient to internal and external shocks.

———————